THE DROWNING GIRLS

COMRADES

THE DROWNING GIRLS
BETH GRAHAM, CHARLIE TOMLINSON, DANIELA VLASKALIC

COMRADES
DANIELA VLASKALIC, BETH GRAHAM

PLAYWRIGHTS CANADA PRESS
TORONTO • CANADA

LIBRARY AND ARCHIVES CANADA CATALOGUING IN PUBLICATION
Graham, Beth
The drowning girls ; & Comrades / Beth Graham, Charlie Tomlinson, Daniela Vlaskalic.

Contents: The drowning girls / Beth Graham, Charlie Tomlinson, Daniela Vlaskalic -- Comrades / Beth Graham, Daniela Vlaskalic.
ISBN 978-0-88754-847-5

1. Smith, George Joseph, 1872-1915--Drama. 2. Sacco, Nicola, 1891-1927--Drama. 3. Vanzetti, Bartolomeo, 1888-1927--Drama. I. Tomlinson, Charlie II. Vlaskalic, Daniela III. Title. IV. Title: Comrades.

PS8613.R343D76 2009   C812'.6080351   C2009-901459-9

Playwrights Canada Press acknowledges that we operate on land which, for thousands of years, has been the traditional territories of the Mississaugas of the New Credit, the Huron-Wendat, the Anishinaabe, Métis, and the Haudenosaunee peoples. Today, this meeting place is still home to many Indigenous people from across Turtle Island and we are grateful to have the opportunity to work and play here.

We acknowledge the financial support of the Canada Council for the Arts—which last year invested $153 million to bring the arts to Canadians throughout the country—the Ontario Arts Council (OAC), the Ontario Media Development Corporation, and the Government of Canada for our publishing activities.

Canada Council   Conseil des arts
for the Arts   du Canada

ONTARIO ARTS COUNCIL
CONSEIL DES ARTS DE L'ONTARIO
an Ontario government agency
un organisme du gouvernement de l'Ontario

CONTENTS

INTRODUCTION

Everyone loves a wedding.

In 1999, audiences at the Bride of Frankenfringe, the eighteenth annual edition of the Edmonton Fringe, were startled to see two brides in full white wedding regalia disappear into a pair of claw-foot tubs.

The venue was Catalyst Theatre. And the far-from-blushing brides emerged, sodden and dripping, back from a watery grave to chant—with a certain cheerfulness—a sort of duet catalogue of destinations, both classic and inventive, for fellow corpses. Iceboxes, meat pies, suitcases, trash bins, cellars, tubs of acid.... This macabre list went on, with special emphasis on death by drowning. *The Drowning Girls* was, as far as I know, the first time in Canadian theatre that Percy Shelley, Ophelia, Dennis Wilson of the Beach Boys, and the passengers on the *Titanic* had ever been referenced in the same scene.

The waterlogged brides, it turned out in the course of this odd and original fantasia, had been married, briefly, to a real-life Edwardian opportunist named George Joseph Smith, who drowned a succession of his short-term wives, with new insurance policies, in the bathtub during the early years of the last century. "Undressed, undone, and underwater, all in a month," said one, with a certain rueful wit.

Fringe buzz, the most electric means of communication at Edmonton's monster summer festival, jump-started *The Drowning Girls*. Audiences flocked to the debut theatrical experiment devised by a couple of University of Alberta acting grads, Beth Graham and Daniela Vlaskalic (who both donned the bridal white), and one of their professors, Charlie Tomlinson (who directed). For one thing, audiences, including me, were struck by the complex tone of the new play, a certain playfulness, even whimsicality, in the face of dark, no, gruesome subject matter.

A notorious serial-murder tale, which might have invited a narrow moralistic optic—killing women is bad; so are psychos—was the aquatic playground, instead, for speculation about a female mystery. How could these women have been duped into acquiescing, fatally, in Smith's monstrous crimes? How could they not have noticed his transparent lies? How could they have allowed themselves to become estranged from their families, and from common sense?

The result was something of a group portrait of a culture: women in a man's world. The contemporary topicality, though never bludgeoned (or drowned), floated free of the period setting.

But even more, perhaps, audiences were drawn to the blithely offbeat theatricality of *The Drowning Girls*. In addition to splashes of H_2O, and a certain quirky Victoriana, the piece gave off waves of *eau de Fringe*. Its insights were inseparable from its striking visual aesthetic and its performance style. As a debut for a trio of collaborators, two of whom spent the whole show soggy, it was auspicious, to say the least.

The Fringe, then and now, is a laboratory for theatre artists with an exploratory bent and the *chutzpah* to take a leap into left field—where people try things they don't know in advance if they can do. Graham and Vlaskalic, trained actors, notably skilled and fresh from theatre school, wouldn't have called themselves playwrights at the time. But they were keen to collaborate on something new, a performance piece they would create, for themselves, from scratch. Vlaskalic came across the story of George Joseph Smith, with its eerie, half-lit puzzle of the wives, and their apparently limitless pliability when it came to "a man of independent means." She and Graham enlisted the versatile Tomlinson, an actor himself, as well as director and writer.

And *The Drowning Girls* was born, in a fortuitous double-image image: a bathtub filled with water. So was a new and adventurous chapter in the lives of its actors/creators: a playwriting partnership that went on to *Comrades* the very next year (directed by Tomlinson), as well as *For Ever For Always, The Last Train* (which won the 2003 Alberta Playwriting Competition), and *Mules*—and continues to this day.

That hit premiere production of *The Drowning Girls* did its bit for the Bride of Frankenfringe's box office dowry (1999 ticket sales were the highest ever in twenty-eight annual editions of the Fringe). And it scooped up a Sterling Award as Outstanding Fringe Production. More than that, though, the rebirth and subsequent successes of the piece tapped directly into a certain Fringe oxygen, the liberation of the acting brigade from working on "other people's plays" in favour of creating and performing original work. Image and performance based, and developed collaboratively, it is cited frequently as an inspiration by actor co-ops with bright ideas—particularly since *The Drowning Girls* didn't expire after the Fringe.

Too often, a Fringe premiere is also the final curtain for the experiment. I'd hate to admit how often I've erroneously predicted an extension of the Fringe into the "season" proper. *The Drowning Girls* is a rare and warming example of artists capitalizing on what they learned in the course of their original investment. In 2008, fully eight years after its original outing, Graham, Vlaskalic, and Tomlinson revisited their inaugural piece. They fashioned a new full-bodied, full-length version of *The Drowning Girls*: two acts, three actors (Graham, Natascha Girgis, Vanessa Sabourin), three claw-foot tubs. The newly refitted play ran at the 2008 pylayRites Festival at Calgary's Alberta Theatre Projects, then returned home to Edmonton to drench the Catalyst stage under the Bent Out of Shape Productions imprimatur.

The undertow of multiple seductions, marriages, and watery demises is now amplified by the slightly older Margaret (Girgis), desperately on the brink of spinsterhood, and married but a single day before her fatal aquatic "misadventure." Narratively, of course, three has a more serial rhythm than two, as befits the subject matter, with its practised villain. Just when the protean predator, Smith, had fine-tuned his homicidal technique, he misstepped, and got caught.

The script included in this volume is both expanded and tightened, the perspective afforded by an eight-year hiatus between drafts. Suspense, the dimensionality of the characters, the sense of a corseted world with its own rules... all are enhanced by the major rewrites—without losing the quixotic tone, the wit, the strange lightness that are the signatures of the piece. The most explicit anachronisms have been eliminated; Dennis Wilson, for example, is returned to pop culture. But the modern implications are clear for anyone who has ever been "swept off their feet," abandoned herself, and later wondered exactly what she'd been thinking.

The production, seen by both Calgary and Edmonton audiences, was deluxe. Ladies and gentlemen, I give you... plumbing! The world of three doomed brides, who enthusiastically, joyfully, embraced their fates ("a woman needs to be married"), was evoked in a stunning, stylized design. The dark, surreal lustre of the original theatrical imagery, enhanced by a trio of designers—Bretta Gerecke (set), Narda McCarroll (lighting), Peter Moller (sound)—included three outsized tubs with overhead showers on a stage of gleaming bathroom tiles.

The birth and evolution of the show into its current seaworthy form, ready to be handed over to actors other than its creators, says something buoyant and important about the Fringe itself, and the uses to which the festival's invitation to experiment is put by developing artists. The same thing is true of *Comrades*. The Jazz Age two-hander premiered at the 2000 Fringe with co-authors Graham and Vlaskalic, cross-gender, in the lead roles of Nicola Sacco and Bartolomeo Vanzetti.

This time, a seminal historical crime captured the imagination of the pair, thanks to Tomlinson, who brought it to their attention. The 1920 murder trial and subsequent execution seven years later of two Italian immigrant labour activists counts as one of the most outrageous frame-ups of the twentieth century. Even at the time it looked manufactured. Later, the names Sacco and Vanzetti, the shoemaker and the fish peddler, would come to define an era, martyrs to American xenophobia and paranoia, sacrificed on the capitalist altar, targeted for their renegade political views.

Emblems of a terrible and rampant injustice, the pair has inspired novels, films, poems, songs, and plays. Sacco and Vanzetti's prison correspondence, amounting to hundreds of surprisingly eloquent letters, along with trial transcripts, became the fabric of the new Graham/Vlaskalic play. Sacco and Vanzetti's ringing declarations on behalf of free speech and workers' rights are woven into the play, which surrounds them with the flavours of an era, its excited high spirits and its jagged cutting edges.

When the Edmonton co-op Kill Your Television Theatre, specialists in the raw and gritty, took up the script in 2008, Graham and Vlaskalic revisited *Comrades*. They amplified it into full-length form; their characters gained dimensions as arrivals in a new-found land that was meant to be an inspiration for the oppressed everywhere.

Not long after the revival of *The Drowning Girls* at Catalyst came Kevin Sutley's elegant production of *Comrades* in the same venue, starring Kevin Corey as Sacco and Nathan Cuckow as Vanzetti, both powerful performances. And it suddenly became clear, some eight years after its original airing, that *Comrades* wasn't merely a series of galvanizing declarations in a doomed cause; it was a fully fleshed play about the immigrant experience—the cruel disillusionment with the "idea" of America, the fear of the outsider in a land of outsiders.

And, as in the case of *The Drowning Girls* in its post-Fringe life, Sutley's production of *Comrades* was beautifully conceived to evoke rather than explain. Kerem Cetinel's design, copper-railed on two levels, conjured a ship, the queues at Ellis Island, the prison cell where injustice and disappointment, amazingly, never caused Sacco and Vanzetti to renounce their belief in America.

Like fatal diseases, blatant injustice has a way of overtaking drama. And trials are plays in themselves, with their own rules of inevitability. The beauty of both *Comrades* and *The Drowning Girls* is that contemporary resonances are powerful, but they are neither pasted on nor explained. Both have a political sense. Feminist incredulity emanates from one; political outrage from the other. McCarthy and Abu Ghraib, chilling names, linger unspoken in the sepia ambience of *Comrades*.

But there's an emotional fullness to the account of female desperation in *The Drowning Girls*, and to the account of bewildered idealism in *Comrades*, with its story of two hopeful arrivals in the land of the free and the home of the brave.

Graham and Vlaskalic discovered something about their multi-faceted talents at the Fringe. And they've discovered something too, about artistic momentum. All there for you to discover in this volume, with its hints of theatrical rewards still to come.

Liz Nicholls, 2009

THE DROWNING GIRLS

BETH GRAHAM, CHARLIE TOMLINSON, DANIELA VLASKALIC

ACKNOWLEDGEMENTS

The playwrights thank Bob White, Dianne Goodman, and everyone at Alberta Theatre Projects; Eva Cairns, Jonathan Christenson, and everyone at Catalyst Theatre; Vicki Stroich, Amy Lynn Strilchuk, Marian Brant, Patrick Fraser, James DeFelice, Gie Roberts, Adrienne Smook, Kira Bradley, Michele Brown, The Citadel Theatre, and Vern Thiessen.

The playwrights acknowledge the crucial support of the Canada Council for the Arts, the Alberta Foundation for the Arts, the Edmonton Arts Council, and the assistance of the 2007 Banff Playwrights Colony—a partnership between the Canada Council for the Arts, the Banff Centre, and Alberta Theatre Projects.

The Drowning Girls toured nationally from 2009–2011. The play went to the Tarragon Theatre (Toronto), the Royal Manitoba Theatre Centre (Winnipeg), the Persephone Theatre (Saskatoon), the Citadel Theatre (Edmonton), the Gateway Theatre (Richmond), and the Belfry Theatre (Victoria) with the following company:

BESSIE	Daniela Vlaskalic
ALICE	Beth Graham
MARGARET	Natascha Girgis

Director: Charlie Tomlinson
Co-designers: Bretta Gerecke and Narda McCarroll
Composer and Sound Designer: Peter Moller
Stage Manager: Lindsay McIntosh and Cheryl Millikin
Technical Director: Patrick Fraser

○ ○ ○

The Drowning Girls premiered at the Alberta Theatre Projects on March 6, 2008, as part of the Enbridge playRites Festival of New Canadian Plays with the following company:

ALICE	Beth Graham
BESSIE	Vanessa Sabourin
MARGARET	Natascha Girgis

Director: Charlie Tomlinson
Co-Designers: Bretta Gerecke, Narda McCarroll
Composer and Sound Design: Peter Moller
Dramaturge: Dianne Goodman
Stage Manager: Amy Lippold
Apprentice Stage Manager: Carla Ritchie
Artistic Director: Bob White
Director of Production: Lance Olson
Technical Director: Darrell Shaw

The original version of *The Drowning Girls* premiered at the 1999 Edmonton International Fringe Festival with the following company:

ALICE   Beth Graham
BESSIE   Daniela Vlaskalic

Director: Charlie Tomlinson
Stage Manager: Erica Letchford
Designer: Cherie E. Hoyles

This version was subsequently produced by Bent Out of Shape Productions at:

Pick of the Fringe, Theatre Network, September 1999
The New Varscona Theatre, May 13, 2000
On the Waterfront Festival, Dartmouth, Nova Scotia, May 2000

Also produced by Let it Land Theatre for the 2000 Ottawa Fringe Festival.

Characters

BESSIE also plays GEORGE, CAROLINE, JOHN, Dr. BILLINGS, Mrs. RAPLEY, AMELIA, MARKS, and Sergeant PAGE.

ALICE also plays JOHN, GEORGE, HENRY, Mrs. TUCKETT, Mrs. CROSSLEY, JANE, Inspector NEIL, and Mr. BODKIN.

MARGARET also plays HENRY, the CONDUCTOR, Alice's MOTHER, Mrs. BLATCH, Sergeant REID, KNOWLES, the CONDUCTOR, and Miss BRIGHTON.

ACT ONE

○ ○ ○

Darkness. A harmonium plays.

BESSIE emerges from her bathtub clutching a bar of soap, gasping, trying to catch her breath.

A gasp from ALICE as she emerges from her bathtub.

BESSIE   Alice?

ALICE crawls out of the tub coughing, spluttering, and laughing.

BESSIE and ALICE perform a synchronized swimming routine. They take a huge breath in and dunk their heads into their bathtubs. They try to stay under water as long as they can, legs flailing in the air. ALICE loses and BESSIE begins a new game.

BESSIE   She was found under the floorboards.

ALICE   She was found with her throat cut.

BESSIE   Found in a suitcase.

ALICE   Found with a mouth full of arsenic.

BESSIE   Found chopped to pieces,

ALICE   then baked in a pie.

BESSIE   Found tied to a tree in Hyde Park.

ALICE   Found bricked up behind a wall.

BESSIE   Found bound with a rag in her mouth.

ALICE   Found at the bottom of the stairs.

BESSIE   Found dissolved in a tub of acid.

ALICE   Found frozen in an icebox.

BESSIE   Found crushed under carriage wheels.

ALICE   Found set on fire.

BESSIE   Found in the trash.

ALICE   Found stabbed in the heart.

BESSIE   Found in a mattress.

ALICE   Found stomped to death.

BESSIE   Found under water

ALICE   used

BESSIE   broken

ALICE   and discarded.

BESSIE   Found?

ALICE   Found?

> *MARGARET emerges gasping.*

MARGARET   Drowned.

> *Silence. BESSIE and ALICE climb into their bathtubs. A moment of coldness. A knock.*

BESSIE   Just a minute, Henry.

ALICE   Just a minute, George.

MARGARET   Just a minute, John.

BESSIE   What will this night bring?

ALICE   Married six weeks.

MARGARET   Married a day.

BESSIE   Married a time.

ALICE   My mouth kissed.

MARGARET   His hands.

BESSIE   My foot touched,

ALICE   patted

MARGARET   tickled. *(She giggles and the others laugh.)*

I love you.

BESSIE   I love you.

ALICE   I love you.

MARGARET   I remember...

BESSIE   on the bridge,

ALICE   at the chapel,

MARGARET   a park bench.

BESSIE   Raining.

ALICE   A kettle boiling.

MARGARET   A fountain.

BESSIE   Proposing.

ALICE   BE

MARGARET   MY

BESSIE   WIFE!

ALICE   Yes.

MARGARET   Yes!

BESSIE   YES!

A gasp as they grip their tubs.

MARGARET   Head wrenched back,

ALICE   eyes wide,

BESSIE   bulging.

MARGARET   His eyes—

ALICE   no words,

BESSIE   mouth shut.

MARGARET   Filling up,

ALICE   going under,

BESSIE   submerging.

ALICE   Darkness.

BESSIE   Silence.

MARGARET   Eternally.

They slide down into the bathtubs. A knock.

ALL   Just a minute.

They surface, reading newspapers.

BESSIE   Beatrice Constance Annie Mundy. Born August twenty-fourth, eighteen hundred and seventy-nine.

ALICE   Alice Burnham. Born December first, eighteen hundred and eighty-seven.

MARGARET   Margaret Elizabeth Lofty. Born April seventeenth, eighteen hundred and seventy-six.

BESSIE   Found...

ALICE   Drowned...

MARGARET   In her bath.

BESSIE   Thirteenth of July.

ALICE   Twelfth of December.

MARGARET   Eighteenth of December.

BESSIE   1912.

ALICE   1913.

MARGARET   1914.

BESSIE   Mrs. Henry Williams.

ALICE   Mrs. George Joseph Smith.

MARGARET   Mrs. John Lloyd.

BESSIE   Aged thirty-three.

ALICE   Aged twenty-six.

MARGARET   Aged thirty-eight.

BESSIE   Married for a time.

ALICE   Married six weeks.

MARGARET   Married a day.

BESSIE   Died unexpectedly—

ALICE   Died suddenly—

MARGARET   Died tragically—

ALL   —on Saturday.

> *ALICE remains in her tub reading the newspaper. BESSIE*
> *and MARGARET climb out of their tubs and bring ALICE her*
> *wedding dress.*

ALICE   I don't want to. Do I have to?

BESSIE   Yes.

ALICE   It doesn't make any sense.

MARGARET   Nothing ever does.

BESSIE   It makes perfect sense.

MARGARET   Step into it.

ALICE   Who says I have to?

BESSIE   Doctors.

MARGARET   Lawyers.

ALICE   Fathers.

BESSIE   Hold still.

ALICE   It's not fair.

MARGARET   That's the way things are.

BESSIE   What do you expect?

ALICE   But why?

BESSIE   We're women.

> *ALICE is dressed.*

ALICE   Can't vote. Can't own property. Can't show an ankle. Can't
have an opinion. Can't breathe in this dress.

BESSIE   That's the way the world is.

ALICE   Can't wear pants.

BESSIE   Why would you want to?

ALICE   Can't say leg.

MARGARET   Alice!

ALICE   Or arm.

MARGARET   Alice!

BESSIE   You must call it a limb.

ALICE   We can't do anything that isn't ladylike? Can't, can't, can't. I'm so sick of being a lady.

BESSIE   You'll be happy when you're married.

BESSIE rushes to get her dress.

ALICE   Yes, yes, I know. We have to be married.

BESSIE   Don't you want to?

BESSIE holds up her dress. MARGARET and ALICE help her put it on.

ALICE   I don't want to be a burden to my family,

MARGARET   a ladies companion,

BESSIE   a lonely spinster aunt.

MARGARET   One of those women walking alone,

BESSIE   in a shabby dress,

ALICE   going home to shabby boarding houses.

Daniela Vlaskalic, Natascha Girgis, and Beth Graham
photo by Cylla von Tiedemann

MARGARET   A ladylike gentility.

BESSIE   Without a home,

ALL   no family to call my own.

ALICE   To go on, being practical and careful and prudish and boring.

MARGARET   To be pitied

ALICE   and cast aside.

BESSIE   What about love?

> *BESSIE is dressed and MARGARET goes to get her dress.*

ALICE   If I'm going to get married I want to be in love.

MARGARET   Consider yourself lucky if you get married at all.

> *MARGARET puts on her dress alone.*

ALICE   I'm going to find a man, any man.

MARGARET   It's not up to you.

BESSIE   We have to wait.

ALICE   How long?

BESSIE   Until someone asks you.

MARGARET   What happens if no one asks you? What if no one wants you? Then you'll remain one of those women; shunned, unwanted, and forgotten.

> *MARGARET is dressed.*

ALICE   But that didn't happen.

MARGARET   No, it didn't.

BESSIE   I dream about my wedding. I can't wait for it. My special day, when I'm the centre of attention. A life of respectability, of acceptance, a useful member of society. I welcome people to my home, entertain guests. Talk to my friends about our children and husbands, the possibilities are endless.

ALICE   But that didn't happen.

BESSIE   No, it didn't.

MARGARET   But it could have.

BESSIE   How do I look?

ALICE   Beautiful.

ALL   The happiest day of my life.

> *They live in their perfect reverie.*
>
> *A sharp sound and they turn to see GEORGE.*

MARGARET   Oh.

BESSIE   There he is.

ALICE   Yes.

MARGARET   We'll be all right. Just breathe.

ALICE   He's changed.

BESSIE   He's not the way I remember him.

ALICE   Shorter.

MARGARET   Unkempt.

BESSIE   Miserable.

ALICE   I don't want to look at him.

MARGARET   Don't worry, he can't see us. Well… shall we?

ALICE   I suppose.

BESSIE   I was just starting to have fun.

MARGARET   Let's do this.

> *They catch their breath and exhale.*

ALICE   In each case the woman is considered vulnerable.

> *The song "Tea For Two" by Vincent Youmans and Irving Caesar plays as they set up tea in the bathtub.*

BESSIE   How was your trip?

ALICE   Unbelievable. I don't even know where to begin.

BESSIE   Where did you go? What did you do? I thought you were going to Southsea.

ALICE   I was in Southsea.

MARGARET   Nothing exciting happens in Southsea.

BESSIE   It's not where you are. It's who you're with.

ALICE   Exactly. You'll never believe—

BESSIE   I was in Clifton visiting my aunt.

MARGARET   How is she?

BESSIE   Oh, fine. The same.

ALICE   All alone, poor thing.

MARGARET   Feeling badly for her won't do her any good.

ALICE   No one to look after her.

BESSIE   Margaret, where did you go?

MARGARET   To Bristol.

BESSIE   And how was the weather?

MARGARET   Seasonable.

> *They all sip their tea.*

BESSIE & ALICE   I met a man!

> *They look at each other.*

MARGARET   So did I.

> *They look at MARGARET in disbelief.*

ALICE   Do tell.

> *Pause.*

BESSIE   Well?

ALICE   Come on, Margaret.

BESSIE   Don't keep us guessing.

MARGARET   I met him in Bristol.

ALICE   And?

BESSIE   Did you ask if he was…

MARGARET   I won't make that mistake again.

ALICE   We all make mistakes.

BESSIE   What does he do?

MARGARET   He's a man of independent means.

     They all laugh.

BESSIE   And how old is he?

MARGARET   The same as me.

ALICE   Is he funny?

MARGARET   He makes me smile.

BESSIE   How does he make you feel?

MARGARET   Enough questions.

BESSIE & ALICE   How did it happen?

MARGARET   He came up to me in the park when I was taking in the evening air. I was sitting on a bench and he sat down on the far end of the same bench. We sat for a long time in silence and then it just poured out of me. Everything, every last detail.

ALICE   You told a stranger everything?

BESSIE   That doesn't sound like you.

MARGARET   Everything.

ALICE   And what did he say?

MARGARET   Nothing, he just listened and looked at me, and I felt understood.

BESSIE   I'm so happy for you.

MARGARET   I felt he knew me.

BESSIE   And you, Alice, who did you meet?

ALICE   A devil.

MARGARET   Don't you ever learn?

ALICE   I met him in church.

MARGARET   Church?

BESSIE   Oh dear.

ALICE   Yes, in church, we were singing "Nearer My God to Thee."

MARGARET   I've always disliked that song.

ALICE   There was a man standing across from me as we sang. Baritone. He kept looking at me. Staring.

BESSIE   How daring.

MARGARET   How rude.

ALICE   We were all taking tea in the rectory. I kept looking around for him but he was nowhere to be seen. Then from behind me, "May I get you another cup of tea?"

BESSIE   What did you say?

ALICE   "Have we met somewhere before?"

MARGARET   You're very bold.

ALICE   That's how he made me feel.

BESSIE   What did he say?

ALICE   "I don't think so. I'm certain I'd remember you." I laughed and we left.

BESSIE   Together?

MARGARET   What then?

ALICE   Then we walked and we talked and we laughed for hours.

BESSIE   I met a man, too. On the bridge, high up above the Avon Gorge. Halfway across, I see him standing, leaning on the rail, looking at the view. He's content. Standing in the afternoon rain without an umbrella. I'm surprised that I'm so aware of him. I am just past him, the moment lost, when he straightens up and spins around. I drop my package. "I'm so sorry," I say. He bends down, picks up the package, and says,

MARGARET & ALICE   "I didn't mean to startle you."

BESSIE   He touches my arm. I fall into step beside him. We walk to the end of the bridge together and continue walking and talking for hours.

ALL   For hours.

MARGARET   In each case the woman was swept off her feet.

ALICE   How could I say no?

BESSIE   Nothing to hold on to.

MARGARET   Impossible to resist.

BESSIE sits on the tub.

MARGARET becomes HENRY and puts a ring on BESSIE'S finger.

HENRY   A token of my love.

BESSIE   This burning passion and sweet desire that I feel for you has made my stomach weak, my head hot. You touch me and I tremble. You come near me, I can't think. The idea of you means I can't sleep, I can't eat, I can't breathe…

HENRY drops her into the tub.

BESSIE becomes GEORGE.

GEORGE   Alice, I've got something for you.

ALICE   What is it?

GEORGE   Say please.

ALICE   Please, George.

GEORGE teases ALICE with the ring.

GEORGE   Will you?

ALICE   Will I what?

GEORGE   Take a chance, Alice.

ALICE   But it's only been two weeks.

GEORGE   Be mine.

ALICE   Oh George, when I'm here with you, surrounded by you, all there is, is you. George, George, George!

GEORGE   Take a chance.

ALICE   Yes, yes. You've made me the happiest woman in the world!

ALICE screams with delight, runs around, and sticks her head under water, still screaming.

MARGARET sits on the edge of the bathtub and waits.

ALICE and BESSIE become JOHN.

MARGARET   Husband?

JOHN   I know this seems quick.

MARGARET   Two days.

JOHN   But when I'm sure of something, I'm sure.

MARGARET   Two days.

JOHN   I have feelings for you.

MARGARET   John.

JOHN   I know you have feelings for me, too.

MARGARET   Yes.

JOHN   Life is too short.

MARGARET   I know.

JOHN   Why waste time?

MARGARET   It's true.

JOHN   You don't have to worry anymore. I'll take care of us, I'll take care of you.

MARGARET   But John…

JOHN   I'll take you to London. I'm opening a business there.

MARGARET   John, slow down.

JOHN   You'll be taken care of. Be my wife.

MARGARET   Yes, yes, yes.

> *MARGARET puts the ring on her finger.*

> *The women pick up their buckets and exchange them as gifts.*

ALICE   Freedom.

BESSIE   Love.

MARGARET   Last chance.

ALICE   *(giving her a bucket)* Bessie…

BESSIE   Thank you so much, Alice.

MARGARET   Oh you shouldn't have.

ALICE   Tall.

BESSIE   Dark.

MARGARET   Handsome.

ALICE   Baritone.

BESSIE   Strong features.

MARGARET   Shy.

ALICE   Good teeth.

BESSIE   Military bearing.

MARGARET   Understanding.

ALICE   Athletic build.

BESSIE   Masterful.

MARGARET   Reserved.

ALICE   Dangerous.

BESSIE   Romantic.

MARGARET   Kind.

ALICE   Lean.

BESSIE   Dashing.

MARGARET   *(giggling)* Long feet.

ALICE   Funny.

BESSIE   Brave.

MARGARET   Intelligent.

ALICE   Eligible.

BESSIE   Good listener.

MARGARET   Large hands.

ALICE   Protector.

BESSIE   Provider.

MARGARET   Saviour.

ALICE   Friend.

MARGARET   Companion.

BESSIE   Prince Charming.

ALL   Husband.

BESSIE   Controlling.

MARGARET   Unfeeling.

ALICE   Cold-hearted.

BESSIE   Hypocrite.

MARGARET   Cruel.

ALICE   Rough.

BESSIE   Abusive.

MARGARET   Callous.

ALICE   Ruthless.

BESSIE   Merciless.

MARGARET   Pitiless.

ALICE   Thief.

BESSIE   Cheat.

MARGARET   Fraud.

ALICE   Bigamist,

BESSIE   liar,

ALICE   predator,

BESSIE   killer,

ALL   executioner.

A wedding march plays.

BESSIE   In each case a counterfeit marriage takes place.

MARGARET   Isn't she lovely?

ALICE   What a beautiful bride!

BESSIE   I always cry at weddings.

MARGARET   She's too good for him.

ALICE   She deserves to be happy.

BESSIE   Shhh, I like this part.

ALICE   I wanted it.

BESSIE   I needed it.

ALICE   My sister already married.

MARGARET   Calling me an old maid.

BESSIE   A woman needs to be married

MARGARET   or you'll grow old alone.

ALL   A man to stand by your side.

MARGARET   Something old.

> *MARGARET puts on a necklace.*

> *They all dash water on their necks and chests as though it were perfume.*

ALL   Oooh! Ahhh!

> *In the bathtub they discover stockings.*

Ahhh! Something NEW!

> *They begin to put on their stockings.*

BESSIE   I wanted romance.

ALICE   I wanted to be swept off my feet.

MARGARET   I just wanted someone.

BESSIE   I was in love with love.

ALICE   It was now or never.

BESSIE   So charming.

ALICE   So distinguished. Who invented these things anyway?

MARGARET   A man of independent means.

They giggle.

BESSIE   Something borrowed?

BESSIE finds a handkerchief.

MARGARET   Accepted at last,

BESSIE   whole,

ALICE   free.

BESSIE   Hurry up. Hurry up.

MARGARET   Calm down.

ALICE   Ready.

They stand, ready.

ALL   The happiest day of our lives.

They put on their veils and get into their bathtubs.

The brides of the bathtub.

ALICE   Something blue.

They all find blue bouquets of flowers.

MARGARET   Marry in blue,

ALL   lover be true.

BESSIE   I, Beatrice Constance Annie Mundy,

ALICE   I, Alice Burnham,

MARGARET   I, Margaret Elizabeth Lofty,

BESSIE   take thee, Henry Williams,

ALICE   George Joseph Smith,

MARGARET   John Lloyd,

BESSIE   to be my lawfully wedded husband,

ALICE   to have and to hold,

MARGARET   in sickness and in health,

BESSIE   for better, for worse,

ALICE   for richer, for poorer,

MARGARET   from this day forward,

ALL   until death do us part.

> *The wedding march warps. Water showers down on them.*

BESSIE   Office of the registry in Weymouth.

ALICE   Portsmouth registry office.

MARGARET   Office of the registry in Bath.

BESSIE   No flowers.

> *They let the flowers fall.*

ALICE   No guests.

MARGARET   No prayers.

BESSIE   No music.

ALICE   No poetry.

MARGARET   No dance.

BESSIE   "No fuss."

ALICE   "Affordable."

MARGARET   "Simple."

> *They slowly start sinking into their bathtubs.*

BESSIE   Just the way he liked things.

ALICE   Say this.

MARGARET   Sign that.

BESSIE   Over and done with before you've had a chance to catch your breath.

ALL   The Drowning Girls.

> *They pop up.*

ALICE   In the beginning there was an insurance salesman

MARGARET   and a woman and they had a-a—aaagghhhh!

> *MARGARET and ALICE act out the birth of GEORGE.*

ALICE & MARGARET   It's a boy!

A baby cries.

BESSIE   And they named him

ALICE & MARGARET   George Joseph Smith.

BESSIE   George becomes the nine-year-old stealing fruit from a barrow boy.

MARGARET   "Apples, get your apples."

ALICE (as GEORGE) steals an apple.

ALICE   Swipe!

MARGARET   "Hey you, that's my apples!"

ALICE (as GEORGE) runs away and is apprehended by BESSIE.

BESSIE   And was sent to reformatory until the age of sixteen. Once out, he speedily took to evil courses, stealing from his own mother.

ALICE   Steal!

ALICE (as GEORGE) steals money from MARGARET.

Natascha Girgis, Daniela Vlaskalic, and Beth Graham
photo by Cylla von Tiedemann

MARGARET   "George, dear, that's my money."

> *ALICE (as GEORGE) laughs.*

> *BESSIE pretends to ride a bicycle. ALICE (as GEORGE) pushes BESSIE off and rides away on the bike.*

ALICE   Shove! Grab!

BESSIE   "Hey you, that's my bicycle."

> *ALICE (as GEORGE) rings a bike bell and laughs.*
> *MARGARET apprehends GEORGE.*

MARGARET   "Six months hard labour!"

BESSIE   Only his mother comes to visit him.

MARGARET   "Oh, George dear, you've broken my heart."

BESSIE   And then the lost years, 1902–1908.

ALICE   *(marching)* Perhaps a soldier in the Northampton Regiment.

BESSIE   *(marches over and screams in GEORGE's face)* "Smith! You horrible little man. The best part of you ran down your mother's leg!"

> *ALICE (as GEORGE) shakes in her boots and pees herself.*

"And clean up that mess."

"And drop and give me ten!"

MARGARET   Or a gym instructor.

> *MARGARET flexes and grunts.*

ALICE   *(as she paddles a boat)* Or a travelling salesman, crossing the Atlantic,

BESSIE   unfortunately not on the *Titanic.*

ALICE   Then transforming himself from the youth into the lover.

BESSIE   The red-hot lover.

MARGARET   Hubba, hubba.

ALICE   Seducing maids to steal from their employers.

MARGARET   "Look what I have, George."

BESSIE   "Anything for you, George."

ALICE (as GEORGE) gets thrown in jail.

ALICE   And again the jailbird, sentenced to twelve months for larceny and receiving. Three cases in all.

BESSIE   "Womanizer."

MARGARET   "Bastard."

ALICE   "You good-for-nothing, lazy, low-life."

ALICE (as GEORGE) escapes.

MARGARET   Then the free man, selling sweets in Leicester. Caroline Thornhill, with her sweet tooth, thinking him to be her sugar daddy, takes a bite and marries her Mr. Love.

BESSIE   "I do. I do. I do."

MARGARET   But the sweet shop fails.

BESSIE   "I think I have a cavity."

ALICE   Then the married man becomes the marrying man because why work when you can steal from your wives? First, Miss Freeman.

MARGARET   "You have laid siege to my heart."

BESSIE   He took her for two hundred and sixty pounds, and then he took her to the National Art Gallery where he left her—

ALICE   "Excuse me, my dear, I need to see a man about a horse."

BESSIE   —in front of a Turner painting entitled *Yacht Approaching Cowes.*

BESSIE holds up the painting.

BESSIE & ALICE   *(looking at the painting)* Wow. *(turning to the audience)* Wow.

MARGARET   "I returned to our rooms, opened the door, and there was nothing there. He had taken everything. He left me with nothing but three empty boxes and the clothes on my back."

BESSIE   And then there was another town, another would-be bride, Ms. Wilson.

"Yoo hoo."

MARGARET   Meets Mr. Smith, a man of independent means,

They all laugh.

ALICE   "Yoo hoo!"

MARGARET   who relieves Ms. Wilson of her life savings,

ALICE   "I can take care of the money for you, my dear, you have no pocket."

MARGARET   and disappears into the traffic of the Franco-British Exhibition.

ALICE hides.

BESSIE   "He went away to get a paper and never came back. What he had taken consisted of the whole of my life savings."

ALICE   Next, the art dealer,

MARGARET   calling himself Henry Williams, meets,

BESSIE   Beatrice Constance Annie Mundy.

Looking out over the sea at Clifton,
wondering if this is all that life has in store,
taking tea, reading and walking along the promenade,
an endless rolling, waiting…
for what?

The crowds of holidaymakers surrounding me,
the cheerful wives, the laughing children,
the husbands enjoying their families.
I walk as one alone, shunned, unwanted, and discreetly pitied.
My father's hand from the grave controlling my money,
still treating me as though I were a child,
not to be trusted.

BESSIE inhales.

It was as if I could suddenly breathe,
as if all my life I had been holding my breath,
and with one look at him my lungs filled with air
and my heart began to beat.

The world turned upside down,
I saw everything differently,
enjoyed the feeling I get when other women saw us together.
No longer the solitary lady,

shunned and ignored by the matrons of Clifton,
now desired and treasured by a man of means and property,
a man of the world!

I was amazed at the effect a wedding ring had upon my entire
existence.

> *ALL sigh.*

Wedded bliss.

MARGARET   It's like...

ALICE   It's like...

BESSIE   It's like dancing.

> *They all do a deep curtsy to the "man" in front of them.*

I'd be delighted.

ALICE   I'd love to.

MARGARET   Very well.

> *They rise and extend their hand to the "man" in front of them.*

BESSIE   I'm trembling.

MARGARET   I thought you'd never ask.

ALICE   This is going to be fun.

> *A waltz begins to play. They dance.*

BESSIE   Happiness.

MARGARET   We don't need words.

ALICE   Perfectly in step.

MARGARET   Am I dreaming?

BESSIE   Paradise.

MARGARET   He never treads on my toes,

ALICE   or steps on my dress.

MARGARET   Too good to be true.

BESSIE   Pure bliss.

MARGARET   I feel light-headed.

ALICE   I know. Isn't it wonderful?

MARGARET   I think I need to sit down. The bliss has gone to my head.

> *MARGARET releases her "man."*

BESSIE   Are you all right, Margaret?

ALICE   You don't know what you're missing.

MARGARET   Alice, be careful, he's a devil.

ALICE   Oh, I know what I'm getting myself into.

MARGARET   Away you go, then. Around and around you go.

BESSIE   Be careful, Alice.

> *ALICE spins out of control and falls.*

MARGARET   I think that's enough.

BESSIE   Let's keep dancing.

ALICE   I got carried away. You keep dancing, Bessie.

BESSIE One, two, three… one, two, three…. I can do this. I can do this.

> *MARGARET begins keeping time.*

MARGARET   That's right, follow his lead.

BESSIE   All this love, where do I put all this love?

> *ALICE begins keeping time with MARGARET.*

MARGARET   One week married.

BESSIE   My other half—

ALICE   Two weeks married.

BESSIE   —my better half. At the flower shop they called me Mrs. Williams. Mrs. Henry Williams. I love you. I love you. I love you.

MARGARET   Three weeks married,

ALICE   and he abandons her.

> *MARGARET and ALICE become HENRY.*

MARGARET   "Dear Bessie,"

ALICE   "I fear you have blighted all my bright hopes of a happy future."

MARGARET   "I have caught from you a disease, which is called the bad disorder."

ALICE   "For you to be in such a state proves to me you cannot have kept yourself morally clean."

MARGARET   "I don't want to say you have had connections with another man and caught it from him."

ALICE   "There is no mistake. I must go to London."

MARGARET   "For the sake of my health and honour."

ALICE   "The bad disorder is not easily cured."

MARGARET   "It's going to cost a great deal of money."

ALICE   "It may take weeks, months, even years before I am cured."

MARGARET   "Your loving husband."

BESSIE   Henry?

ALICE   "Bessie."

BESSIE   Yes?

ALICE   "If your family comes, what are you going to say?"

BESSIE   That you've left for France on business.

MARGARET   "And if your uncle comes?"

BESSIE   I'll tell him the truth.

MARGARET   "And what is the truth?"

BESSIE   That I've given you the bad disorder.

> ALICE and MARGARET turn their backs on BESSIE.

Don't go. Please. Whatever I did wrong, I'm sorry. I'm so sorry. I don't want to be…. I can't. I can't. I can't.

> BESSIE walks to the bathtub, kneels down, grips the sides. She takes a deep breath then exhales all the air and plunges her head under the water.

> ALICE becomes Mrs. TUCKETT.

BESSIE   (coming out of the water with the bouquet of blue flowers) Oh, Mrs. Tuckett!

TUCKETT   Yes?

BESSIE   Mrs. Tuckett!

TUCKETT   Coming!

BESSIE   Mrs. Tuckett!

TUCKETT   What?!

BESSIE   Oh, Mrs. Tuckett,the most wonderful thing has happened! I met my husband on the way to pick up your flowers. He's come back!

TUCKETT   What in heaven's name are you talking about?

BESSIE   When I left the house this morning, I decided to walk along the seawall. I thought the salt air would lift my spirits a little. And there he was, looking out over the water.

TUCKETT   I hope you pushed him in.

BESSIE   I touched his arm and he turned to me and said, "All a mistake."

TUCKETT   What?

BESSIE   Oh Mrs. Tuckett, it was a like a dream. He has spent the last year looking for me.

TUCKETT   But he knows your relatives and knows where they live. Why didn't he ask them?

BESSIE   Henry said they wouldn't tell him. But he found me anyway. All on his own.

TUCKETT   Miss Mundy, take a breath.

They both take a breath.

Bessie, think carefully. Think back to when he left you and how upset you were. You wouldn't leave your bed and your brother had to go and fetch you. Your uncle sent you here to board with me, and I feel responsible for you.

BESSIE   Have no fear, Mrs. Tuckett. I feel I now know my husband better than I ever did before.

TUCKETT   He lied to you, he deserted you, he stole your money from you, and he said that you had given him the bad disorder.

BESSIE   He intended to pay it back all along.

TUCKETT   The hell he did.

BESSIE   It's all behind us now.

TUCKETT   It's not just the money. It's your reputation, the way he treats you.

BESSIE   He's explained everything to me and wants things to be as they were.

TUCKETT   But Miss Mundy—

BESSIE   Henry said that you would try and come between us.

TUCKETT   You silly girl.

BESSIE   I'm sorry, Mrs. Tuckett, but I am leaving.

TUCKETT   You can't possibly—

BESSIE   I'm leaving.

TUCKETT   Miss Mundy—

BESSIE   I'm Mrs. Williams!

> *A knock.*

I have to go. He's waiting for me.

TUCKETT   What about your things?

BESSIE   I'll send for them.

TUCKETT   No, promise me you'll come back tonight to get them. I want to meet this husband of yours.

BESSIE   Fine. Goodbye.

> *A moment between the two women.*

I suppose that I may go with my husband now?

> *BESSIE goes.*

MARGARET   Three days later, a letter.

TUCKETT   Dear Madam,

In consequence of the heated argument you had with my wife, and for the sake of peace, we have decided to stop away and remain together as man and wife. As far as Bessie and I are concerned, the past is forgiven and forgotten. I trust there are many years of happiness before us. I thank with all of my heart all those who have been kind to my wife during my absence.

Yours respectfully,

H. Williams

> *Mrs. TUCKETT steps forward as though she were giving evidence.*

It was as if she didn't hear a word I said. She left with him, without taking any of her belongings. She promised to come back that same night, but I never saw her again.

BESSIE   Better to have loved and lost than to have never loved at all.

I had often heard that true love would make you go blind.
I never believed.
I cared nothing for the money.
I would have given it all to him if only... if only... if only.

Innocent, faithful, devoted,

ALICE   naive, blind, foolish,

MARGARET   obliging, quiet, Christian,

ALICE   pathetic, duped, frustrated,

MARGARET   incompetent, artless, guileless,

ALICE   imprisoned, enslaved, pitiable,

MARGARET   tragic, lonely, hopeless, wealthy.

BESSIE   That's who I was, according to the court records and the newspapers.

But I really don't recognize myself in that,
I don't remember.
I do know that I married Henry Williams and I was happy for a time.

> *Water showers down into the three bathtubs.*

ALICE   In each case all the woman's ready money is realized.

BESSIE   I've drained my savings account.

MARGARET   I've emptied my purse.

ALICE   The last of my wages.

MARGARET   Here you are, John.

BESSIE   Here you are.

ALICE   Here.

BESSIE   All my belongings.

MARGARET   My jewellery.

ALICE   Anything for you, George.

BESSIE   Anything for you.

MARGARET   Anything.

BESSIE   My inheritance, twenty-five hundred pounds.

MARGARET   All of it.

BESSIE   Everything.

ALICE   Every last penny.

> *The showers stops.*

MARGARET   In each case the woman is isolated from her family. Mr. Smith, apparently still irresistible to women and in need of funds, meets the twenty-six-year-old Miss Alice Burnham in Southsea. She takes him home to meet her family.

> *Sound of a train.*
>
> *BESSIE becomes GEORGE.*
>
> *ALICE and GEORGE are on a train travelling to Aston Clinton. GEORGE is reading a newspaper.*

ALICE   Read it to me again, George.

GEORGE   Mr. and Mrs. Charles Burnham of Aston Clinton, announce the engagement of their daughter, Miss Alice Burnham, to Mr. George Joseph Smith, son of George Thomas Smith. A December wedding is planned. Miss Burnham is a nurse and Mr. Smith is a man of independent means.

ALICE   I wish they hadn't written that last part about me being a nurse.

GEORGE   That part of your life is over.

ALICE   I can't wait. I've asked mother to arrange the chapel. You'll love it.

GEORGE   Anything you love, I love.

ALICE   Oh, George. You're going to love mother. Father may take a while to warm up to, but I know you'll get on. Are you nervous? You shouldn't be.

GEORGE   As long as I have you by my side. I've already written them a letter introducing myself and telling them how much I adore you.

ALICE   I wish I could have met your parents, George.

GEORGE   Are you feeling all right, Alice? You look a little flushed.

ALICE   It's all this excitement. It makes me dizzy.

GEORGE   Perhaps you should see a doctor.

ALICE   It's only a headache.

MARGARET   *(as the CONDUCTOR)* "Milton Keynes. Next stop, Milton Keynes."

ALICE   George, we're here.

    The scene shifts. BESSIE becomes Alice's FATHER.

FATHER   ALICE! Alice, come here!

    MARGARET becomes Alice's MOTHER.

MOTHER   Alice, don't go.

ALICE   If George is not welcome here, then neither am I.

MOTHER   Please, be reasonable.

ALICE   Father hasn't been. He never gave George a chance. He disliked him from the start. He said he was "evil."

MOTHER   Well George hasn't acted very respectfully. He was so rude at dinner when your father asked about his family.

ALICE   He was being interrogated.

MOTHER   Alice, he said his mother was a bus horse, his father a cab driver—

ALICE   Yes, yes, I know, and his sister a roughrider over the arctic regions. He was joking.

MOTHER   It was rude.

ALICE   Father was being a bully.

MOTHER   Do you think it's unreasonable that your father is concerned about whom his daughter is marrying?

ALICE   He can be concerned without being mean.

MOTHER   We don't know anything about his background or his family.

ALICE   I'm not marrying his family.

MOTHER   Let me talk to your father again.

ALICE   What's the use?

MOTHER   Your father is a good judge of character.

ALICE   I don't want to get married here.

MOTHER   Alice, this is all so hasty—

ALICE   We love each other.

MOTHER   You've only known him two weeks.

ALICE   Can't you see that I am finally happy.

MOTHER   I don't want to see you hurt. Be practical, we raised you to be practical.

ALICE   To be practical and careful and prudish and boring. That's why you don't understand George. He's so different from this stifling house.

MOTHER   You're being childish.

ALICE   I'm twenty-six years old.

MOTHER   Alice, your father—

ALICE   —doesn't understand—

MOTHER   —loves you.

ALICE   I'm leaving, Mother.

MOTHER   Alice.

ALICE   What?

MOTHER   *(She gives ALICE a necklace.)* Something old.

ALICE   Will you come to my wedding?

MOTHER   I can't. Your father wouldn't have it.

ALICE   Goodbye, Mother.

MOTHER   Please write and tell me all about it. Let me know how you are doing… you can always come back.

ALICE   With George?

ALICE sinks into the bathtub.

MOTHER   A letter arrived shortly after Alice left. It was addressed to my husband.

Sir,

The views and actions which you have been pleased to take towards our marriage are both inconsistent and contemptible. Having failed in your attempt to wreck all possibilities of marriage, you take shelter in obdurateness, contempt, and remorse…. I am not going to waste my time in trying to enlighten you on things you are quite old enough to understand, but lest I remind you that causing friction, as you have, is the greatest mistake in your lifetime.

G. J. S.

MOTHER steps forward, as though giving evidence.

They were married two weeks later. I never saw my daughter alive again.

MARGARET turns and sees ALICE in the bathtub.

BESSIE   In each case the woman's life is insured.

BESSIE becomes MARKS. MARGARET becomes KNOWLES.

KNOWLES   Mrs. Smith?

ALICE   Who?

MARKS   You are Mrs. Smith?

KNOWLES   Aren't you?

ALICE   Yes?

MARKS   And how is your

MARKS & KNOWLES   husband?

ALICE   What?

KNOWLES   Your husband.

MARKS   George

KNOWLES   Joseph

MARKS   Smith.

ALICE   Oh yes. Mr. Marks, or is it Mr. Knowles?

MARKS   *(together)* I'm Marks. He's Knowles

KNOWLES   *(together)* I'm Knowles. He's Marks.

MARKS   We've had a letter,

KNOWLES   from your father,

MARKS   saying that he will pay the money

KNOWLES   that you say he owes you.

ALICE   All of it?

MARKS & KNOWLES   Yes, we have the cheque.

ALICE   And the interest?

KNOWLES   Yes.

MARKS   Four pounds,

KNOWLES   one shilling,

MARKS & KNOWLES   and one penny.

ALICE   Thank you.

MARKS & KNOWLES   And the life insurance policy?

> *Cashier bells go off.*

ALICE   Oh yes.

MARKS   Your life insurance policy,

KNOWLES   Mrs. Smith,

MARKS   that your husband asked us to prepare.

ALICE   Yes, George said, "A life insurance policy with a few premiums paid up is a valuable asset.

ALL   One can even borrow on it in times of need

ALICE   and feel secure in the knowledge that those you leave behind will be provided for."

KNOWLES   Did your husband discuss effecting an insurance policy on his own life?

ALICE   Yes, he promised to get one sometime about his next birthday.

MARKS   When the rates are more favourable.

MARKS & KNOWLES   Good.

KNOWLES   That is the common and fair practice between married people.

MARKS   So... *(calculating)* is five pounds annually acceptable as the premium on this policy?

ALICE   Yes.

KNOWLES   Do you have that amount with you?

ALICE   Yes, I've just taken out all my life savings from the bank to give to my husband.

       Water showers down.

How foolish was I?

Undressed, undone, and under water
all in a matter of months.
A whirlwind romance.
Swept off my feet.

How could I not have known?

I go over the events again and again in my mind,
replaying everything.
If only...

BESSIE   if only...

MARGARET   if only...

ALICE   No. As soon as I met him, there was only the one way.
There, with him,

MARGARET   surrounded,

BESSIE   by him.

ALL   All there was, was him.

ALICE   How foolish was I?

Well I let him take me away from my family.

BESSIE   Yes?

ALICE   I'm not marrying his family.

MARGARET   No.

ALICE   My life was insured for one thousand pounds.

MARGARET   Yes...

ALICE   I paid the premium myself!

BESSIE   Right.

ALICE   My will was drawn up—

MARGARET   Then?

ALICE   I gave everything to George.

BESSIE   Ah.

ALICE   How foolish was I? Well...

BESSIE   I got into the bath.

MARGARET   I got into the bath.

ALICE   I got into the bath.

ALICE jumps out of the bathtub.

BESSIE   In each case there are unnecessary visits to a doctor.

MARGARET   He convinced me I was having seizures

BESSIE   and convulsions,

ALICE   that my headaches were serious,

MARGARET   and I needed medical attention.

ALICE   Alice, you are so beautiful.

BESSIE   Bessie, you are so precious to me.

ALICE   Alice, you are so lovely.

ALICE & BESSIE   Margaret, you are so ill.

BESSIE and ALICE are waiting to see the doctor.

MARGARET   Is this right for Dr. Billings?

BESSIE and ALICE nod.

I hate waiting at the doctor's.

BESSIE ignores her and lifts her newspaper.

I don't know why I have to come here. I feel perfectly fine.

ALICE ignores her and lifts her newspaper.

But my husband insists.

ALICE and BESSIE become JOHN.

ALICE   "Margaret, you've had a fit."

BESSIE   "You were shaking violently."

MARGARET   Was I?

BESSIE   "Go and see a doctor."

ALICE   "Better safe than sorry."

Silence.

MARGARET   He said I fell down and was shaking. I don't remember.

BESSIE   I don't remember.

ALICE   I don't remember.

MARGARET   What's wrong with me? Nothing. For the first time in my life I'm happy.

BESSIE becomes Dr. BILLINGS and gets into the bathtub.

BILLINGS   Mrs. Lloyd?

MARGARET   Doctor Billings?

BILLINGS   What seems to be the matter?

MARGARET   My husband thought I should come and see you. He said I had some sort of fit last night. My husband thinks that it might be epilepsy.

BILLINGS   Do you remember ever having had fits in the past?

MARGARET   No.

BILLINGS   What about nausea? Hot flashes? Hysteria? Irrational
behaviour? Fits of uncontrollable weeping? Flying into a rage at
the slightest and most trivial provocation? Inclination to morbid
thoughts? Insane hatred of the male gender? Or any of the
innumerable ailments to which your sex are prone?

MARGARET   I have been blessed with an excellent constitution.

BILLINGS   Take a breath. Did you experience twitching limbs, moving
jaw, or a dreadful scream?

MARGARET   I don't remember.

BILLINGS   Exhale. What did your husband say?

MARGARET   John told me that I lost consciousness and that my limbs
were twitching.

BILLINGS   How long did this fit last?

MARGARET   My husband said only a few moments and then I fell into
such a deep sleep that he couldn't wake me. But when I woke up this
morning I couldn't remember any of it.

BILLINGS   Inhale. How old are you?

MARGARET   I'm thirty-eight years old.

BILLINGS   Exhale. The probability of a woman having her first
epileptic fit at thirty-eight is very unlikely.

MARGARET   Is that what you think, Doctor?

BILLINGS   Inhale. Are your parents still living?

MARGARET   No.

BILLINGS   Exhale. Do you ever recall them having had any "fits"?
Follow this.

> BILLINGS swings the "something old" necklace in front of
> MARGARET's eyes.

MARGARET   No, but my father suffered from excessive nervousness.
Could it be hereditary?

BILLINGS   Do you ever feel excessively nervous?

MARGARET   Sometimes.

BILLINGS   Well, Mrs. Lloyd, I suggest that you try to not worry and to not indulge your overly active and fanciful female imagination with ideas of dementia and bedlam.

MARGARET   *(tearing up)* Is there something wrong with me?

BILLINGS   Here.

> BILLINGS *hands her the "something borrowed" handkerchief.*

MARGARET   Thank you.

BILLINGS   It's only a slight fever, perhaps a touch of influenza. There's nothing to worry about.

MARGARET   But I don't remember.

ALICE   You will.

BESSIE   You will.

MARGARET   How did it all happen so quickly?

I barely had time to catch my breath.

Married a day.

I know, I know, I shouldn't have—
I'd resigned myself. I wasn't afraid.
I accepted my situation.
I wasn't expecting him. I was surprised.

ALICE   Ambushed.

BESSIE   Willing. Tuesday,

MARGARET   I met him in the park. He gave me proofs of his—

ALICE   Wednesday,

MARGARET   he brought all his paperwork and suggested we be married. I only did what thousands have done—

BESSIE   Thursday,

MARGARET   I agreed. Kept it all a secret, even from my sister.

Dear Elsie,

I'm off to the station. I go to meet the lady I am looking after. Hope to see you soon. Do not worry. I am well and happy. Sorry not to have been able to tell you before, but it was all arranged so quickly. I've had barely any time to think.

Your affectionate sister.

ALICE   Friday,

MARGARET   married and went to the bank.

BESSIE   On Saturday,

MARGARET   saw a doctor, went to the lawyer's, and—

ALICE   *(as JOHN)* "You'll feel better after you've had a bath."

MARGARET   He hasn't left my side, not even for an instant. He even made sure they had a bath here.

>   *MARGARET gets into the bathtub.*

Alone, for the first time this week.
What am I doing? How…? Is this what I've always wanted?
I don't know him. I'm out of my depth.
This isn't you, this is someone else… Mrs. Margaret Lloyd?

>   *A knock.*

BESSIE   In each case a will is made in the husband's favour.

MARGARET   Last will and testament of Margaret Elizabeth Lofty… Lloyd.

ALICE   I, Alice Smith, declare this to be my will and testament and I revoke all prior will and codicils that I have made.

BESSIE   I am married to Henry Williams, and in the event of my death, I give my property all to my spouse.

MARGARET   Isn't that what a married couple does?

BESSIE   It didn't take long, he had nothing. I had everything.

ALICE   It was the gesture that mattered.

MARGARET   He did all the talking. I just sat there and nodded.

ALICE & BESSIE   What else were we supposed to do?

MARGARET   In each case letters are written the night before death extolling the husband's kindness.

> *BESSIE, ALICE, and MARGARET kneel and write the*
> *following letters on the floor.*

BESSIE July 12, 1912.

ALICE December 11, 1913.

MARGARET December 17, 1914.

BESSIE Dear Uncle,

ALICE Dear Mother,

MARGARET Dear Sister,

Last Thursday night I had a bad fit.

ALL I lost consciousness and my limbs were twitching.

MARGARET I have been provided with the best medical man here,

ALL who is attending on me day and night.

MARGARET My husband has done everything he could for me

ALL and has been extremely kind.

MARGARET I have made my will

ALL and left all I have to my husband,

MARGARET this is only natural,

ALL as I love my husband.

MARGARET Yours affectionately,

ALICE From your daughter,

BESSIE I remain yours…

> *An intake of breath, as they exhale they sign, saying their*
> *names aloud, all at once.*

Mrs. Beatrice Constance Annie Williams.

ALICE Mrs. Alice Smith.

MARGARET Mrs. Margaret Lloyd.

> *They leap to their feet.*

BESSIE Dr. French!

ALICE Dr. Bates!

MARGARET   Dr. Billings!

BESSIE   My wife is dead.

ALICE   My wife cannot speak to me.

MARGARET   My wife is under the water.

They run to their bathtubs.

ALICE   In each case the husband inquires about a bath.

BESSIE   In each case the husband is the first to discover the body.

MARGARET   In each case the husband pretends to be on an errand at the time of death.

The landladies arrive.

BESSIE becomes Mrs. RAPLEY. ALICE becomes Mrs. CROSSLEY. MARGARET becomes Mrs. BLATCH.

They each take a bucket and start cleaning.

RAPLEY   Have you heard?

CROSSLEY   I know, I know. I can't believe it myself.

RAPLEY   They were sleeping just upstairs.

BLATCH   I really don't want to talk about it.

RAPLEY   When did you first see him?

CROSSLEY   They just came in on the train and were looking for a place to rent.

RAPLEY   She looked so happy.

BLATCH   Haven't you got anything better to talk about? What about poor Mrs. White and her gout?

RAPLEY   You never want to talk about it.

BLATCH   Don't speak ill of the dead.

CROSSLEY   Poor thing didn't see it coming.

BLATCH   None of them saw it coming.

Pause. Scrubbing.

RAPLEY   We went to look at the room upstairs and I heard him mumble something to her.

CROSSLEY   What was it?

RAPLEY   I don't know, but she turned to me and said, "Oh yes, have you a bath?" and I said, "Yes, I do."

CROSSLEY   I didn't have a bath, so he brought one in.

They all shake their heads in disbelief.

BLATCH   What happened next?

RAPLEY   I put towels and soap in the bathroom and run the bath. I go downstairs and hear her go into the bathroom and close the door. I hear the tap shut off.

CROSSLEY   I'm sitting in the kitchen. I see the water coming through the ceiling and dripping down the walls.

BLATCH   I hear a sound of splashing. There's a noise, as if someone is putting wet hands or arms on the side of the bath and then a sigh. The sigh is the last I hear.

CROSSLEY   Then the bastard sat down and played the harmonium. He went on and on and on.

RAPLEY   Why do you suppose he played that song? "Nearer My God to Thee."

BLATCH   I don't want to talk about it.

CROSSLEY   That's how he got his jollies.

RAPLEY   I think he was making his peace with God.

BLATCH   Let's get on with it.

CROSSLEY   Sing us a verse.

The song is sung badly, half-remembered, and muttered as they clean.

RAPLEY   *(singing)* Nearer, my God, to Thee, nearer to Thee!

CROSSLEY   *(joining in)* E'en though it be a cross that raiseth me,

ALL   Still all my songs shall be, nearer, my God, to Thee.

BLATCH   Nearer, my God, to Thee,
Nearer to Thee!

Pause.

RAPLEY   Then it got quiet.

CROSSLEY   Very, very quiet.

BLATCH   Silent as the grave.

A knocking at the door.

RAPLEY   I go to see who it is, and there he is, nervous and out of breath.

CROSSLEY   Bold as brass.

BLATCH   Cool as a cucumber.

RAPLEY   And he says to me, "I went to get some fish for my wife's supper."

CROSSLEY   And he expected you to cook it, I suppose.

RAPLEY   Yes, and he pushed it at me and walked on upstairs.

The landladies look up.

CROSSLEY   "Forgot my key," he said with a straight face.

RAPLEY   Where'd he been?

CROSSLEY   "I've brought these flowers for my wife, would you put them in some water." Then he went up the stairs.

The landladies look up again, listening.

BLATCH   He was standing there smiling at me. "Sorry to disturb you, my dear Mrs. Blatch, but I seem to have mislaid my key." Then he took out a tomato and placed it in my hand and gave it a squeeze. Winked at me and bounded up the stairs. I think he was whistling.

RAPLEY   He called out.

CROSSLEY   What did he say?

RAPLEY   "She is dead."

CROSSLEY   "Fetch the doctor. My wife cannot speak to me."

BLATCH   "She's in the bath, come and help me."

RAPLEY   I found her naked, clutching a bar of soap.

CROSSLEY   I covered her up with a sheet.

BLATCH   I didn't want her looking at me.

CROSSLEY   You're not going to believe this?

RAPLEY   What? What?

CROSSLEY   He returned the bathtub, saying, "This thing's no good, it killed my wife."

RAPLEY   *(knocking on the tub)* Seems all right to me.

CROSSLEY   Buried on the cheap.

RAPLEY   No mourners.

BLATCH   No marker.

CROSSLEY   No questions asked at the inquest.

RAPLEY   No marks on the body.

CROSSLEY   No signs of a struggle.

RAPLEY   No suspicious circumstances.

BLATCH   Death by misadventure.

CROSSLEY   Asphyxia from drowning.

RAPLEY   Had a fit in her bath.

BLATCH   No foul play.

ALL   Scott free. Tsk. Tsk. Tsk.

> *CROSSLEY steps forward and gives evidence.*

CROSSLEY   After the funeral, he came to fetch his suitcase and stayed for about ten minutes. I remember him leaving me an address on a postcard. I wrote on the back; wife died in bath, I shall see him again someday.

> *MARGARET becomes Alice's MOTHER. BESSIE becomes AMELIA, Alice's sister.*
>
> *It is one year to the day since ALICE's death. They have just returned from burying Alice's father.*

AMELIA   Shall I get Jane to make us some tea?

MOTHER   Yes, please.

ALICE becomes JANE, the maid.

AMELIA   Jane, would you be so kind as to bring us some tea?

JANE   *(bobs)* Yes, ma'am… and may I offer my deepest condolences on the loss of Mr. Burnham.

MOTHER   Thank you, Jane. It was a beautiful funeral. Please tell everyone the flowers were lovely. It was very kind of them.

JANE   *(bobs)* Yes, ma'am. I'll get your tea now.

JANE leaves.

AMELIA   Should I come home and stay with you for a while?

MOTHER   No dear, get back to your children. Life is for the living.

AMELIA   You'll be very lonely here, Mother. What will you do?

MOTHER   Think.

AMELIA   Father wouldn't want you here on your own.

MOTHER   Maybe I'll end up just like him and die of a broken heart.

AMELIA   Please don't say that.

MOTHER   He was never himself again after Alice died.

AMELIA   I know.

MOTHER   I never thought I would have to bury any children of mine.

AMELIA   I can't imagine. *(pause)* It's been a terrible year for us, Mother. First Alice's death.

MOTHER   A year ago today.

AMELIA   You're right, how terrible, and Papa's funeral on the self-same day.

MOTHER   Your father never liked that man, never trusted him, not for an instant. Remember how he wouldn't allow him to sleep under our roof when he visited, and Alice stormed out.

AMELIA   And was married two weeks later.

MOTHER   I never saw my daughter alive again.

JANE   *(calling)* Ma'am, ma'am.

> *JANE enters with a newspaper, giving it to MOTHER and pointing at an article. MOTHER reads.*

MOTHER   Amelia, Amelia, read this.

> *MOTHER gives AMELIA the newspaper and pulls another newspaper article out of her own pocket, or perhaps she has memorized the article. As they recite the articles ALICE sinks into her bath.*

AMELIA   *(reading the article)* Mrs. John Lloyd.

MOTHER   Mrs. George Joseph Smith.

AMELIA   Aged thirty-eight.

MOTHER   Aged twenty-six.

AMELIA   Married a day.

MOTHER   Married only six weeks ago.

AMELIA   Bride's Tragic Fate on Day after Wedding.

MOTHER   Bride's Sudden Death.
Drowned after seizure in a hot bath.
Both recently married.

MOTHER & AMELIA   On Saturday.

AMELIA   They're the same.
Both had headaches on the train.

MOTHER   Both were taken to a doctor.

AMELIA   Dr. Billings.

MOTHER   Dr. Bates.

AMELIA   Both died by misadventure in her bath.

MOTHER   The heat of the water acted on the heart.

AMELIA   And caused either a fit or a faint, and in her helplessness,

ALICE   drowned.

MOTHER   I think we better call in Scotland Yard.

> *A shift.*

MARGARET   Once is happenstance.

BESSIE   Twice is coincidence.

MARGARET   Three times is suspicious.

BESSIE   The hounds are on the scent!

MARGARET   The cat is out of the bag.

BESSIE   Meow!

ALICE hisses.

ALICE becomes Inspector NEIL. MARGARET becomes Sergeant REID. BESSIE becomes Sergeant PAGE.

They are waiting outside of a lawyer's office. They have staked the place out. JOHN is inside collecting MARGARET's insurance money. The policemen pop up and down from around and inside of their bathtubs.

REID   Blimey! 'E's in there na. Nuff said, yeah?

NEIL   Be careful, dis bastard might 'ave a gun!

PAGE   Ya cover 'is left.

REID   Ya cover 'is wite.

NEIL   Leef the talkin' ter me.

They all pop down. Slowly they peer over the sides of their baths. They make eye contact and pop down again.

PAGE   It'll be good ter lay hands on 'im, sir.

REID   'E's a bad wahn.

PAGE   Why do ya fin' 'e's taken so long ter come for the money?

REID   Busy wif anovver tart.

PAGE   Wot makes 'im do it, sir?

NEIL   Money, me son. It's the root of aw evil.

REID   Makes the world go round.

PAGE   May be that's 'ow 'e gets 'is beef strogonoff.

REID   Drownin' them loike little kittens.

PAGE   How can these birds be so stupid?

REID   Yeah, 'a can they?

NEIL   Aw wite, lads, ter your stations. 'Ere 'e comes. 'Re ya John Lloyd?

PAGE   The geeza agreed that this was 'is name.

NEIL   You were married ter Margaret Elizabef Lofty on December seventeenf last?

PAGE   And she was found dead by ya in a bleedin' bath the followin' bleedin' day?

MARGARET becomes JOHN.

JOHN   "Yes, quite right."

PAGE   'E agreed.

NEIL   Ye 're also said ter be identical wif the same George Smif, whose lovely little trouble and strife, wife, Alice, was found dead in 'er bath under similar circumstances.

PAGE   'E denied it.

JOHN   "Smith? I'm not Smith. I don't know what you're talking about."

NEIL   Any question of further charges is a matter for inquiry.

PAGE   'E kept talkin'.

JOHN   "I must say that the two deaths form a phenomenal coincidence, eh? But that's my hard luck."

PAGE   On the way ter the police stashun Smif admitted,

JOHN   "It is the irony of fate that my two wives should have died in this way."

MARGARET   Fate, John?

ALICE   There's nothing ironic about that, George.

BESSIE   Don't you mean three, Henry?

They address the audience.

ALL   May it please you,

ALICE   it must be noted

MARGARET   that the three cases are of such a character

BESSIE   that the resemblances cannot have occurred

ALL   without design.

ALICE   In Alice's case,

MARGARET   In Margaret's case.

BESSIE   In Bessie's case.

> *MARGARET and BESSIE begin to fill MARGARET'S bathtub with water, as though it were evidence. ALICE measures its depth.*

ALICE   In each case the woman was swept off her feet.

MARGARET   The woman was considered vulnerable.

BESSIE   The woman's life was insured.

ALICE   A counterfeit marriage took place.

MARGARET   The woman was isolated from her family.

BESSIE   All the woman's ready money was realized.

ALICE   The woman made a will in her husband's favour.

MARGARET   The property could only be got at in the event of the woman's death.

BESSIE   There were inquiries about a bathtub.

ALICE   There were unnecessary visits to a doctor.

MARGARET   The husband was the first to discover the woman's body.

BESSIE   There were no signs of violence on any of the victims, no bruises, no lacerations, not even the sounds of a struggle were heard.

> *ALICE becomes Mr. BODKIN. MARGARET becomes Ms. BRIGHTON.*

BODKIN   Gentlemen of the jury, how did he do it? We have brought in a tub of the exact dimensions as the third victim's bath and which is now filled to the same depth. We have asked Ms. Brighton, who is not only a practised swimmer, but also the exact height and weight of the third victim, Mrs. Margaret Lloyd, to assist us by re-enacting her death. Now, Ms. Brighton, you are aware that I am about to attempt to submerge you, if I can?

BRIGHTON   Yes.

BODKIN   And you are accustomed to having your head under water?

BRIGHTON   Oh yes, that is correct.

BODKIN   Ms. Brighton, if you would lie down in the tub, please.

Ms.BRIGHTON shakes her head.

Please.

Ms. BRIGHTON lies down reluctantly in the bathtub and Mr. BODKIN walks over to her.

Now, Miss Brighton, if I were to place my hands on your shoulders and attempt to push you under the water, you would still be able to struggle, yes?

BRIGHTON   Yes.

BODKIN   You would still be able to cry out?

BRIGHTON   Help me!

BODKIN   Very good. If I were to place my hands on your head and try to push it forward and down under the water, you would still have the use of your arms and legs, yes?

BRIGHTON   Yes.

BODKIN   And again you would still be able to cry out, yes?

BRIGHTON   Help me!

BODKIN   Very good. What if I were to reach in, placing my hands under your side, and attempt to flip you over and hold you down?

Mr. BODKIN tries to do this. She fights back, splashing and shouting out.

BRIGHTON   Help me! Help me!

BODKIN   Very, very good.

The degree of violence necessary to overcome the resistance of an adult female who is being drowned in this manner and without anyone hearing is colossal and might I suggest impossible. Which leads me again to ask the question, "How did he do it?"

BESSIE becomes JOHN. Ms. BRIGHTON becomes MARGARET.

The bathroom fills with steam. Sound of knocking.

JOHN   Darling, may I come in?

MARGARET   Yes.

JOHN   Are you feeling better, my dear?

MARGARET   Oh yes, much better.

JOHN   Is the water warm enough?

MARGARET   It's perfect.

JOHN   Are you enjoying your first day as Mrs. Lloyd?

MARGARET   It suits me very well.

JOHN   Let me have the soap. I'll wash your back.

MARGARET   Oh, that feels nice.

JOHN   You look so beautiful in this light.

MARGARET   You are so kind to me, so loving.

JOHN   You make that very easy.

> *JOHN walks to the end of the bathtub and gently takes one of her feet out.*

You have the most delicate feet.

MARGARET   I do not.

> *JOHN tickles her foot and MARGARET laughs.*

JOHN   I love to see you smile.

MARGARET   I love you.

> *He looks at her coldly.*

Is something the matter?

> *JOHN grabs both ankles and swiftly pulls up. They freeze in this pose. JOHN releases MARGARET's legs and then dries his hands with a towel.*

ALICE   The drowning girl would only be under for a few seconds. The force of the water entering her nose and mouth would render her unconscious, unable to struggle or make sound, and eventually lead to asphyxia from drowning.

BESSIE   As her head plunges under the water, what thoughts flood the mind of Margaret Lofty?

ALICE   Or Alice Burnham?

BESSIE   Or Bessie Mundy? Drowning girls, we are told, in the brief space of consciousness left them, review every incident of their lives.

ALICE   What recollections and reflections must have raced through their brains?

BESSIE   Each caress, every tender word,

ALICE   every secret, all the laughter, all rushed back to them in that last crowded moment of consciousness.

> *MARGARET begins to sing "Nearer My God to Thee" from the tub.*

MARGARET   Nearer, my God, to Thee, nearer to Thee!

ALICE   *(joining)* E'en though it be a cross that raiseth me,

BESSIE   *(joining)* Still all my songs shall be, nearer, my God, to Thee

ALL   Nearer, my God to Thee,
Nearer to Thee!
Though like the wanderer, the sun gone down,
Darkness be over me, my rest a stone.
Yet in my dreams I'd be nearer, my God to Thee.
Nearer, my God, to Thee,
Nearer to Thee!

BESSIE   Mrs. Henry Williams.

ALICE   Mrs. George Joseph Smith.

MARGARET   Mrs. John Lloyd.

ALICE   He convinced me to wear this dress.

MARGARET   He convinced me to put on this ring.

BESSIE   He convinced me these stockings were silk.

ALL   They itch!
George Joseph Smith, we accuse you

BESSIE   of being a filthy liar,

ALICE   of playing the harmonium badly,

MARGARET   of being heartless,

BESSIE   of accusing me of giving you a bad disorder,

ALICE   of having no remorse,

MARGARET   of being cold-blooded,

BESSIE   of giving me no respect,

ALICE   of giving me a poor funeral,

MARGARET   of giving me false hope,

BESSIE   of being a consummate scoundrel,

ALICE   of being transparently worthless,

MARGARET   of being a bigamist,

BESSIE   of being a swindler,

ALICE   of behaving with inhuman cruelty,

MARGARET   of being a multiple murderer.

ALL   We rest our case.

BESSIE   The sentence of the court

ALICE   is that you be hanged by the neck

MARGARET   until you be dead.

ALICE   Dead.

BESSIE   Dead.

ALL   And may the Lord have mercy on your soul.

MARGARET   Thirteen steps to the gallows,

BESSIE   the knot is tied,

ALICE   the noose tightens,

ALL   and tightens.

>   *Pause. Water showers down. They all burst out laughing.*

ALICE   Found asphyxiated.

MARGARET   Found suffocated.

BESSIE   Found clutching a bar of soap.

From front to back: Natascha Girgis, Beth Graham, and Daniela Vlaskalic
photo by Cylla von Tiedemann

ALICE   Found

MARGARET   Found

BESSIE   Found

ALL   Drowned.

> *They all lie back into their bathtubs.*

You could say George Joseph Smith took our breath away.

> *Their bodies slip gracefully into the water, laughing, as the music swells and the light fades*
>
> *The End*

Beth Graham, Charlie Tomlinson, Natascha Girgis, and Daniela Vlaskalic
photo by Cylla von Tiedemann

NOTES

The Drowning Girls was inspired by the Scotland Yard case of the notorious murderer George Joseph Smith and his victims, the "brides of the bathtub."

The world of the play is theatrical and non-realistic, created by Bessie, Alice, and Margaret as they piece together the events and present the evidence leading to their deaths. The audience bears witness.

Bessie, Alice, and Margaret are always themselves "playing" characters in their collective story. The women should remain on stage for the entire play, flowing easily from one scene to the next and from character to character. Costume changes are not necessary.

The element of water is essential to the production but not a lot is needed to be effective (a suggested five inches per bathtub is plenty). When working with water, the deck will become slippery, so it is important to have a surface that prevents slipping as much as possible. Another important safety issue concerns the drowning of Margaret at the end of the play. When Margaret is pulled by the feet, her head and shoulders should never go below the surface of the water.

Props should appear and disappear from the tub.

Shower heads above the bathtubs allow for water to come from overhead but are not crucial.

Bessie, Alice, and Margaret should not be played with accents.

This play should be performed without an intermission.

Song: "Nearer My God to Thee" (words by Sarah Adams, 1841, music by Lowell Mason, 1856)

COMRADES

DANIELA VLASKALIC, BETH GRAHAM

ACKNOWLEDGEMENTS

The playwrights thank Charlie Tomlinson; Nathan Cuckow, Kevin Sutley, and everyone at Kill Your Television Theatre; Eva Cairns, Jonathan Christenson, and everyone at Catalyst Theatre; David Beazely, Rylan Wilkie, Massimo Verdicchio, Patrick Fraser, Ashley Wright, Jeff Page, and James DeFelice.

The playwrights acknowledge the crucial support of the Canada Council for the Arts, the Alberta Foundation for the Arts, and the Edmonton Arts Council.

Several books and historical references were significant in the development of this play. Some of these include:

Avrich, Paul. *Sacco and Vanzetti: The Anarchist Background.* Princeton: Princeton University Press, 1991.

Frankfurter, Marion D. and Gardner Jackson, eds. *The Letters of Sacco and Vanzetti.* 1928.

Guthrie, Woody. *Ballads of Sacco and Vanzetti.* B000001DJ0, Smithsonian Folkways. Compact Disc, 1947.

Russell, Francis. *Tragedy in Dedham: The Story of the Sacco-Vanzetti Case.* New York: McGraw-Hill, 1962.

The Sacco-Vanzetti Case, Transcript of the Record, 1920–27 (six volumes). New York: Henry Holt & Co., 1928.

Comrades had its premiere with Kill Your Television Theatre on May 1, 2008. It played at Catalyst Theatre in Edmonton with the following company:

Nicola SACCO   Kevin Corey
Bartolomeo VANZETTI   Nathan Cuckow

Director: Kevin Sutley
Designer: Kerem Cetinel
Composer and Sound Design: Dave Clarke
Stage Manager: Tracey Byrne

An earlier version of *Comrades* premiered at the 2000 Edmonton Fringe Festival with the following company:

Nicola SACCO   Beth Graham
Bartolomeo VANZETTI   Daniela Vlaskalic

Director: Charlie Tomlinson
Stage Manager: Gina Moe

It was produced by Bent Out of Shape Productions and received four Elizabeth Sterling Haynes Award Nominations (Edmonton).

Characters

Nicola SACCO also plays KATZMANN

Bartolomeo VANZETTI also plays Judge THAYER

ACT ONE

★ ★

SACCO and VANZETTI are alone in their separate cells.
They are barefoot and wear only their undershirts, suspenders,
and trousers. VANZETTI writes frantically. SACCO sits,
motionless, staring at his hands. The cell lights flicker.
VANZETTI looks up from his writing, at the light hanging
above him, and SACCO remains as before.

VANZETTI   Nico.

SACCO   …

VANZETTI   I can't stop thinking and writing about everything.

SACCO   …

VANZETTI   August 22, 1927,

The words that I am writing cause my heart to ache.

SACCO   …

VANZETTI   Over and over again, the same words, this heart continues
to beat eagerly. Will anyone read this and understand what is always
in my mind? I hope so. I would like that they should understand what
I am trying to say, and I wish that I could write it more plain. Words
aren't enough.

SACCO   …

VANZETTI   Looking back, I hardly recognize the man I was. So full of
life. Nico?

SACCO   …

VANZETTI   How old were you when you came to this country?

SACCO   …

VANZETTI   I was twenty. A young man.

SACCO   …

VANZETTI   Melancholy won't do us any good.

SACCO   ...

VANZETTI   Do not make life any more miserable.

SACCO   ...

VANZETTI   Do not lose heart.

SACCO   ...

VANZETTI   I know it's not been what you imagined.

SACCO   ...

VANZETTI   America.

> *SACCO laughs.*

The Promised Land.

SACCO   My hands... I don't recognize them.

VANZETTI   The country that was always in our dreams.

> *Flashback to SACCO and VANZETTI as young men. They put on their socks and shoes during the following.*

What is a young man supposed to do in Italy?

SACCO   You are supposed to do what your father does.

VANZETTI   My father wants me to work on the farm. He doesn't think that education is important. He says, "There is no money in books and learning. You must learn a trade to make a living and raise a family."

SACCO   Well my father thinks I'm full of crazy ideas.

VANZETTI   There is no opportunity.

SACCO   No freedom of choice.

VANZETTI   Italy is for the old.

SACCO   And America is for the young.

VANZETTI   I've heard that in America there are libraries with rooms and rooms of books from all over the world.

SACCO   Well I've heard that in America there are carts in the streets loaded with fruits and vegetables, even in February.

VANZETTI   And there is a machine for everything.

SACCO   There is work for anyone willing to work.

VANZETTI   Everyone wears fine clothes, not just the rich.

SACCO   Even the poorest man can make something of himself.

VANZETTI   They say, in America they hand out gold bars when you walk off the ship.

SACCO   Really?

VANZETTI   The cities are filled with buildings so tall they touch the sky.

SACCO   No…

VANZETTI   And women work alongside the men in the factories.

SACCO   Now I know you are lying.

VANZETTI   There is marvellous freedom, freedom of the mind—of ideas. It is all that is modern and enlightened in the world.

SACCO   It is a place where anything can happen. A new world.

VANZETTI   A golden land.

SACCO   A country that is always in my dreams.

VANZETTI   Two more young Italians off to the land of the free.

SACCO   My boots need a polish.

VANZETTI   Not to worry, my pants have holes.

SACCO   I want to look my best. Have you heard about the women in America?

VANZETTI   Help me with my tie.

SACCO   There. Now you look important.

VANZETTI   That's the idea. You've been to the barber.

SACCO   Yes, and even he can't get my hair to lie flat.

VANZETTI   "Don't be ashamed of where you come from."

SACCO   "You must work hard—

VANZETTI   and save money."

SACCO   "Take care of yourself."

VANZETTI   "Don't get into trouble with the ladies."

SACCO   "Or the law."

VANZETTI   "Don't give up too easily."

SACCO   "Remember that you always have a home here."

VANZETTI   "You can always come back."

They shake hands and embrace.

SACCO   When I left my village it was like a death. The girls watched me go, weeping like I was a hero. Some of them even embraced me and I stole as many kisses as I could.

VANZETTI   When my mother died I left my native land, a wanderer without a country.

SACCO   Going to America is like going to the moon.

VANZETTI   The shore is crowded with people: friends, family, strangers, chaos, excitement. Fear of what is to come.

SACCO   I brought a ball of yarn on board the ship, leaving one end of the line with a pretty girl on land. As the ship slowly cleared the dock, the ball unwound amid the farewell shouts of the women, the fluttering of the handkerchiefs, and the infants held high. After the yarn ran out, the long string remained airborne, lost in a maze of yarn, held up by the wind, long after I had lost sight of the girl on shore.

VANZETTI   Farewell to old Italy, the land of my childhood, which now and forever I am going to leave... I'm going to cross over that wide, swelling ocean in search of fame, fortune, and sweet liberty.

A ship's horn sounds.

SACCO   Down below deck in a place meant for animals and freight,

VANZETTI   a place not unlike a prison cell,

SACCO   with little air and little space to move about, we travel.

VANZETTI   Full of hope.

SACCO   Full of dreams.

VANZETTI   Ten days in the foul-smelling hole of an immigrant ship.

SACCO   Some could afford the higher fares that allowed them to travel above deck.

VANZETTI   I never breathed fresh air.

SACCO   I never saw the open sky.

VANZETTI   Oh, I was sick.

SACCO   Oh God, I was sick.

VANZETTI   One night, I prayed the ship would go down because the waves were washing over it.

SACCO   The pitch and roll of wave after wave.

VANZETTI   I thought the old man beside me would die.

SACCO   The old man beside me did die.

VANZETTI   Foul-smelling bodies that haven't bathed in days.

SACCO   The stench of urine and vomit.

VANZETTI   Rats and disease.

SACCO   Choking on smoke from people cooking over an open fire.

VANZETTI   I don't ever want to remember anything about that old ship.

SACCO   As soon as the ship docks, we line up against the rail, anxious to leave.

VANZETTI   There are millions of newcomers pouring in.

SACCO   Then I see her, the most beautiful woman in the world.

VANZETTI   After weeks at sea, we are forced to wait on board for four days.

SACCO   Look at her!

VANZETTI   The passengers are handled by the immigration officials like animals.

SACCO   Do you know what is written at her feet?

VANZETTI   No one says a kind or encouraging word to the newly arrived.

SACCO   "Give me your tired, your poor,
    Your huddled masses yearning to breathe free."

VANZETTI   Little children cling to their mother's skirts, weeping with
    fright.

SACCO   "The wretched refuse of your teeming shore,"

VANZETTI   Until yesterday, I was among people who understood me
    and spoke the same language.

SACCO   "Send these, the homeless, tempest tossed to me,
    I lift my lamp beside the golden door"![1]

VANZETTI   Now I am in a land where my language means little more
    than the pitiful noises of dumb animals.

SACCO   A line of people stretching from the dock to the main
    building.

VANZETTI   We wait, knowing that if we fail the test, we will be sent
    back across the ocean.

SACCO   Why should I fear the fires of hell? I have been through Ellis
    Island.

VANZETTI   Don't wheeze, don't cough, don't shuffle, don't give them
    a reason.

SACCO   They check for cholera.

VANZETTI   For tuberculosis.

SACCO   For epilepsy.

VANZETTI   For anemia.

SACCO   For trachoma.

VANZETTI   "Where did you come from?"

SACCO   "Where are you headed?"

VANZETTI   "Can you speak English?"

SACCO   "Can you read and write?"

VANZETTI   "How much money do you have?"

---

1 An excerpt from *The New Colossus* by Emma Lazarus. The poem engraved on the pedestal
  of the Statue of Liberty.

SACCO   "Do you have a job waiting for you?"

VANZETTI   Some are sent back.

SACCO   But not us.

SACCO & VANZETTI   America.

> *SACCO kisses the ground and VANZETTI picks up a handful of dirt.*

VANZETTI   Maybe dreams do come true in America.

> *The lights flicker and they find themselves back in their cells.*

SACCO   The city dazzled me. I'd never seen such buildings, such people.

VANZETTI   Food—anything you could possibly want. How could a person ever go hungry in this place?

SACCO   So many beautiful women.

VANZETTI   Theatres and museums, libraries, streetcars, everything a person could want… for those who can afford it.

SACCO   In America, there are rooms without sunlight.

VANZETTI   A land of those that have and those that have not. The fat, the lean, the exploiters, and the exploited.

SACCO   It took me two weeks to get work. I was a hard worker, but I couldn't afford to shop in the stores or dine in the restaurants.

VANZETTI I couldn't even afford to live in a clean, comfortable home.

SACCO   Where was America?

VANZETTI   I found work as a dishwasher. A job no one wanted. It was horrible. No windows. Sometimes the electricity failed and we had to open the back door in the dead of winter. But the steam from the dishes still collected on the dirty ceiling and great drops of filthy water fell slowly, one by one, onto my head. The rotting table scraps, collected in a barrel, gave out a nauseating smell, and the sinks overflowed, the water soaking into my shoes as I trudged in slime. I had to leave for fear of contracting consumption.

SACCO   An unskilled labourer is a mat for everyone to wipe their feet on. If my brother and I had come across on the *Mayflower*, things would be different.

VANZETTI   For three months, I walked the streets of New York without finding work. Then Hartford, then Worcester, and finally Plymouth. I couldn't believe the horrible conditions in which people were forced to live and work. Thirty families crammed into a single tenement house.

SACCO   With the cost of rent, how could they afford better?

VANZETTI   Husband and wife working side by side for twelve hours, for three children they never saw.

SACCO   My only escape was the streets. I loved walking in the open air, seeing new people arrive, hearing news from back home. It would give me such a lift to see pushcarts full of fruit and vegetables in the middle of February. That's when I met Rosa. She was buying an orange.

VANZETTI   You found love in America.

SACCO   I could not afford much for my family. I could not put any money in the bank.

VANZETTI   The place where I worked was enjoying extraordinary prosperity because of the war, but none of this made it through to the workers. I lived on fish that I took from the sea. Something needed to change.

SACCO   I should have gone back to Italy with my brother. Then I never would have met Rosa, I never would have—

VANZETTI   But you didn't go back.

SACCO   I stayed because in America I could believe in what I wanted and say what I wanted. I realized too late that promise isn't true.

VANZETTI   We are beaten but we have not yet lost—we may still win.

SACCO   That's impossible.

VANZETTI   I still have hope.

     Pause.

SACCO   How can you write so much and at such a pace?

VANZETTI   It keeps me sane.

SACCO   Don't you ever get tired?

VANZETTI   I must continue the good fight.

SACCO   There's no use.

VANZETTI   Never in our full life could we have hoped to do such work for tolerance, for justice, for man's understanding of man, as we do now by accident.

SACCO   You really believe that.

VANZETTI   With all of my heart.

SACCO   When I saw you for the first time, in that moment, I understood why you were admired and respected. You stood courageously and spoke with such conviction that I listened to your every word. I no longer heard the crowd or the scream of the police sirens. I was mesmerized by you—bound by what you had to say. You spoke so beautifully I could not believe you were speaking in English. I heard my own thoughts and feelings in your words before I had even thought or felt them.

> *The two men are at a rally. VANZETTI reads a flyer that he has written.*

VANZETTI   You have fought all the wars. You have worked for all the capitalists. You have wandered all over the country. Have you harvested the fruits of your labour? The price of your victories? Does the past comfort you? Does the present smile on you? Does the future promise you anything? Have you found a piece of land where you can live like a human being and die like a human being? On these questions, on this argument, and on the theme "The Struggle for Existence," I, Bartolomeo Vanzetti, will speak. Admission free. Freedom of discussion for all. Bring the ladies with you.

> *He hands the flyer to SACCO who takes it and puts it in his pocket.*

SACCO   You speak very well.

VANZETTI   I only say what needs to be said.

SACCO   You are the voice of the workers.

VANZETTI   If only I could convince them to listen and to take action.

SACCO   You don't need to convince me. I already know.

VANZETTI   I'm glad.

SACCO   We are on the brink of a revolution. We must stand together.

VANZETTI   Side by side.

SACCO   They don't believe we will unite, that we will take the risk.

VANZETTI   We will see.

SACCO   *(offering his hand)* Nicola Sacco.

VANZETTI   *(taking his hand)* Bartolomeo Vanzetti.

> *They shake hands.*

SACCO & VANZETTI   Comrade.

> *SACCO and VANZETTI address a crowd at a labour rally.*

VANZETTI   How can a man feed his family on nine dollars a week?

SACCO   How much do you make a week?

VANZETTI   Nine dollars?

SACCO   How much does your wife make?

VANZETTI   Three?

SACCO   Can you feed your family?

VANZETTI   Are there holes in your boots?

SACCO   How many hours in a day do you work?

VANZETTI   When do you clean your house? Feed your children?

SACCO   What do you feed your children?

VANZETTI   Are they hungry?

SACCO   Is this what you left your homeland for?

VANZETTI   Is this your dream?

SACCO   What difference will a five percent increase in your wages make?

VANZETTI   How will you pay for your children's education?

SACCO   Doesn't your child have a right to an education?

VANZETTI   Don't you?

SACCO   If someone in your household is sick, can you afford a doctor?

VANZETTI   Can you afford to miss a day of work?

SACCO   Can you afford to buy medicine?

VANZETTI   Fellow workers! We have made some progress. We have suffered too much already to relinquish what we have gained.

SACCO   If we surrender now, we may as well prepare our neck for the ropes of economic death, which we make with our own fingers.

VANZETTI   In life one needs courage when he faces danger, disaster, starvation.

SACCO   Let us hold on a little longer.

VANZETTI   They need us as much as we need them.

SACCO   *(to VANZETTI)* Do you think they will listen?

VANZETTI   We must continue until they do.

SACCO   What difference will a five percent increase to their wages make? It's like throwing a dog a bone.

VANZETTI   We're so used to being treated like dogs that we're starting to believe that we are.

SACCO   The people seem hopeful. They are tired but in good spirits.

VANZETTI   As long as we stay together. There are rumours of strikes breaking out all over the country.

SACCO   Did you hear in Illinois that the miners gunned down twenty-two strike breakers?

VANZETTI   That won't happen here, this is a peaceful rally. We will not raise a hand against our brothers.

SACCO   If even one of them accepts the offer they could turn on each other.

VANZETTI   We can't back down now.

SACCO   Perhaps the company will make a decent offer.

VANZETTI   We are all gathered here for one purpose—a better way of life.

SACCO   We'll give the company no choice.

VANZETTI   We'll stand together. They will listen.

> *The sound of marching feet, horses' hooves, sirens, and the crowd yelling and screaming. The two men stand horrified, witnessing a violent riot.*

SACCO   The police came and beat us with clubs, like animals. I watched as a woman holding her child was knocked down in the street by a horse and trampled. She called out to me but I could do nothing. I was being held. A young boy, kicked in the stomach, fell down beside me, and as I reached to help him up, I was knocked in the head.

> *The sounds of the riot have died away and SACCO and VANZETTI return to their cells.*

Some of us were taken to cells with no mattresses to spend sleepless nights until they decided to let us go or send us back to Italy. Our protest made little difference.

VANZETTI   How can you say that? The picket line held. The company offered us a wage increase of ten percent.

SACCO   Not nearly enough.

VANZETTI   If only we could have held on a little longer.

SACCO   They forced us to take it.

VANZETTI   But the people saw that change is possible. Ten percent is something.

SACCO   The company could have given more.

VANZETTI   They saw the power of the worker.

SACCO   You were a hero that day.

VANZETTI   All I did was speak my mind.

SACCO   You were blacklisted.

VANZETTI   It was worth it.

SACCO   We were naive to think we could bring down an entire system of government.

VANZETTI   We weren't naive. We were young.

SACCO   Young and foolish.

VANZETTI   "How beautiful is youth! How bright it gleams. With its illusions, aspirations, dreams!"[2]

SACCO   We protested. We were beaten and thrown in jail. Then they give us something to keep us quiet and we accept it.

VANZETTI   The workers were afraid for their jobs, for their families—

SACCO   I have a family, should I have been afraid? Maybe if I had been—

VANZETTI   Should we have done nothing?

SACCO   I wouldn't be here.

VANZETTI   I know you. You're not one to sit by while people suffer.

SACCO   …I keep having the same dream. I am in a mine camp. There is a labour strike for better wages and the masses of workers are impatient and tired of waiting. There are speakers whom the workers are applauding when soldiers come with guns. And so a fight is about to begin when I jump up on a hill in the middle of the crowd and say to the workers, "Friend and comrade and brotherhood, not one of us is going to move a step, and whoever moves will be a coward. Here the fight is going to finish." Then I turn towards the soldiers and say, "Brothers, you will not fire on your own brothers. You know that we fight for freedom, which is your freedom. We want one land, one soul, one house, and better bread." As I say the last word, one of the soldiers fires at me and I watch the bullet pass through my heart and I fall to the ground with my right hand clutching at my chest. Then I wake up with the same old walls staring back at me.

VANZETTI   Nico, one man can make a difference.

SACCO   I went to meetings, distributed literature. I did all this. I talked of nothing but change and what did I get in return? They threatened me and my family with deportation.

VANZETTI   The threat of deportation couldn't stop the storm from coming.

SACCO   "Go ahead and deport us! We will annihilate you in blood and fire. We will dynamite you."[3]

VANZETTI   In all our years of protest we never once spilled a drop of blood.

SACCO   The workers were shown no pity. When a man is persecuted and humiliated sometimes he feels there is no choice but violence.

3 Luigi Galleani

VANZETTI   There is always another choice. The change must be gradual. Anarchists are not so foolish as to believe or to advocate that a government can be changed in a day.

SACCO   We've waited for seven years behind these sad bars.

VANZETTI   By keeping us in here, the Massachusetts court is giving us a good chance to teach the people the true nature of anarchism.

SACCO   I hope the lesson ends soon.

VANZETTI   In the meantime, I will work, I will read, and I will write. *(writing)* On principle, we abhor violence, deeming it the worst form of coercion and authority, but we cannot deny that acts of violence have been committed by men calling themselves anarchists.

    They meet each other on a street corner.

SACCO   I came as quickly as I could.

VANZETTI   I needed to talk to you.

SACCO   Rosa was worried.

VANZETTI   I know it's dangerous.

SACCO   Today, Dante asked me, "What's a wop?" What am I supposed to say to that? What do I tell my son? Then he asks me, "What is a dirty red?" This isn't why I came to this country.

VANZETTI   It's not the same as it was. Everyone is afraid.

SACCO   For ten years, I have worked in this country, and now since the soldiers have come back, since the war has ended, all anarchists are traitors, suspects, Bolsheviks, bombers, wops, and dirty reds.

VANZETTI   They say that all anarchists are violent so that the government can blame us for these latest bombings.

SACCO   That's the problem with government, they can condemn whoever they want.

VANZETTI   They're the ones who are responsible for this uprising.

SACCO   I'm looked at with suspicion and treated as a second-class citizen because I am Italian.

VANZETTI   It's not just because we are Italian. But because we speak out against injustice, they call us radicals, extremists, criminals.

SACCO   They are the criminals, aiding and abetting vigilantes and raiding parties that take people and do God knows what to them. Did you see the paper?

VANZETTI   "Beware the Red Peril."

SACCO   Attorney General Palmer said anyone found with anarchist literature will be immediately arrested and deported.

VANZETTI   He can't do that. A man must be allowed to read what he wants and believe what he wants. He must be given the choice.

SACCO   Not anymore.

VANZETTI   Where will it end? They are out for blood. In Newark, a man was arrested for looking like a radical. Not every immigrant is an anarchist.

SACCO   And not every anarchist is carrying a bomb.

VANZETTI   They hate us because they are afraid.

SACCO   Innocent people are being dragged from their homes in the middle of the night.

VANZETTI   I know.

SACCO   Twenty-five arrests in the last two years in Boston alone. The rumour is that ten thousand foreigners have been deported.

VANZETTI   Nico, the reason I needed to meet… I've just come from Boston. Salsedo…

SACCO   How is he?

VANZETTI   …

SACCO   What's happened?

VANZETTI   He's dead.

SACCO   What?

VANZETTI   He and Elia were arrested and accused of bombings.

SACCO   No.

VANZETTI   Salsedo fell out of a window.

SACCO   Murderers!

VANZETTI   They said suicide.

SACCO   Murderers. What about Elia?

VANZETTI   They're going to deport him. He said they tried to force him to confess, that they beat Salsedo until he wasn't right in the head. It all happened in the middle of the night, and the next morning he was found on the sidewalk fourteen floors down.

SACCO   Oh my God. His family.

VANZETTI   They want to go back to Italy.

SACCO   We'll have to find the money to help them.

VANZETTI   His wife is terrified they're going to come after her.

SACCO   This is a violation of our civil liberties but the people allow it to happen. The press applauds Palmer and his tyranny.

VANZETTI   It's because they don't understand.

SACCO   People need to know the truth about Salsedo.

VANZETTI   I'll write something.

SACCO   But they're planning more raids. If they find us with any literature they will arrest us and deport us, or worse.

VANZETTI   We will have to be careful then.

SACCO   No, it's too dangerous. Too many others have already been deported and now Salsedo is dead. They won't be satisfied until they've gotten rid of all of us. We can't draw attention to ourselves.

VANZETTI   Our comrades need to know what's happened. They need to know they are in danger.

SACCO   Now is not the time. I don't want to find you on a sidewalk fourteen floors down.

VANZETTI   Then we'll collect all of the literature, anything they can use against us, and hide it until things quiet down.

SACCO   We'll need a car.

VANZETTI   Boda. He'll lend us his.

        They shake hands.

SACCO   Comrade.

VANZETTI   Viva l'anarchia.

The lights flicker and a radio broadcast of the South Braintree murder and robbery plays.

RADIO   Frederick A. Parmenter, paymaster, and Alessandro Berardelli, guard, of the Slater & Morrill Shoe Company were gunned down and robbed of the payroll totalling fifteen thousand, seven hundred seventy-six dollars and fifty-one cents, at three o'clock this afternoon. They were shot and killed by two dark-haired foreign men who had been leaning on a fence waiting for them. Immediately after the shooting, a large dark-coloured car moved up the street; the two murderers, with a third man, got into the automobile, which left the scene of the murder and made its getaway. Police are on the lookout for a car matching this description.

Police sirens. VANZETTI and SACCO are in a police car.

SACCO   Why are they arresting us?

VANZETTI   Someone must have told the police.

SACCO   But no one knew that we were collecting the literature.

VANZETTI   Boda knew.

SACCO   He wouldn't turn us in. He was lending us his car, helping us.

VANZETTI   Might have been the woman at the garage. She refused to give us the car. Wouldn't even open the door.

SACCO   We didn't tell her why we needed it. Why would she call the police?

VANZETTI   She must have been afraid. We're foreigners.

SACCO   Anyone caught with anarchist literature will be immediately arrested and deported.

VANZETTI   They have no proof that we've done anything wrong.

SACCO   They found a flyer in my pocket.

VANZETTI   Why didn't you get rid of it?

SACCO   I forgot.

VANZETTI   They can't deport us over a piece of paper.

SACCO   What do we say?

VANZETTI   Tell them your name and where you work. That is all.

SACCO   What if they ask me about my family?

VANZETTI   Say you are nothing but a hard-working man trying to make a life.

SACCO   They're going to separate us and I won't know what to say.

VANZETTI   You don't know me.

SACCO   What?

VANZETTI   You don't know me. You just met me on the streetcar before they arrested us. You don't know Boda, you've never heard of Salsedo, you don't know anyone.

SACCO   I don't know anyone.

VANZETTI   You've never been to any meetings. A stranger gave you that flyer.

SACCO   *(nods)* Thank you, comrade.

VANZETTI   So much for freedom of speech. So much trouble over a piece of paper. We have to protect our friends now.

SACCO   What will you say?

VANZETTI   I will tell them I am an Italian immigrant anarchist.

> *The interrogation begins. SACCO and VANZETTI have been separated and are being questioned. For the first time, they speak with Italian accents.*

SACCO   No, not citizen.

VANZETTI   Why do you say anarchist?

SACCO   Go slow.

VANZETTI   I am a little different.

SACCO   Please.

VANZETTI   Do I like this government?

SACCO   No understand.

VANZETTI   I want things a little different.

SACCO   No, I hate violence.

VANZETTI   I read anarchist papers.

SACCO   Please.

VANZETTI   No, I did not join war.

SACCO   I have wife.

VANZETTI   I did not come to America to be soldier. I am, as you say... conscientious objector.

SACCO   No believe in war. Why should I fight these men? What they do to me?

VANZETTI   You will not make me citizen but you want me to fight?

SACCO   I register, you make me work in labour camp. I have children.

VANZETTI   Why you ask me this now?

SACCO   Why it matter?

VANZETTI   War is over.

SACCO   Stranger gave me flyer.

VANZETTI   People want to speak their minds.

SACCO   I do not know.

VANZETTI   Is it not free country?

SACCO   I do not know him.

VANZETTI   I do not think he know me.

SACCO   What?

VANZETTI   I do not know what you say.

SACCO   I never steal money.

VANZETTI   I never spill blood.

The interrogation ends.

SACCO and VANZETTI return to their cells. Their accents are gone.

SACCO   I long to work, to use my hands. I am not given to reading and writing. I need to be outside because I feel joy when I work. Behind these sad bars, in these dull days, life feels so depressing. Each day, we sit in idleness as the world passes by outside.

VANZETTI   I was just thinking of what I would do to pass the long time in jail. I was saying to myself, "Do some work." But what? "Write," a gentle voice says to me. "Why don't you write something now? It will be useful to you when you are free."

SACCO   I wish you could see us when they come to visit. Dante is quite a boy now, almost as big as his mother, and it seems to me that he loves her very much. Rosa talked about the plays she and I used to perform with the dramatic club to raise funds for strike relief. Rosa never had time to learn her lines, and so she would invent ways to carry her pages with her. One time when she played a nun, she pasted them in a bible, but the pages glued together and so for the rest of the play her nun had taken a vow of silence…. I am very sorry that no one comes to see you. I should send my family. Little Ines is sure to make you smile.

VANZETTI   No… I always find that when the hour given for a visit has passed, I feel that I have more to say than at the beginning of it and so I keep thinking about all the things I didn't say long after they have gone.

SACCO   I was lucky. I had a beautiful wife, a fine son, a sweet daughter, a good, comfortable home, a garden, and a job. How could I have so much and others have so little? In this time of prosperity, men still rummaged in garbage cans for a leaf of cabbage or a rotten potato for their supper. I felt guilt for all that I had.

VANZETTI   I often think of my time selling fish and the independence I felt then when I did not have to answer to anyone. Every morning I would get up at six-thirty and do my rounds. Always, I would start on Cherry Street, where I pick up the fish and make my way down Suosso's Lane, stopping to have coffee with the Brinis, then past the plant at lunchtime, where I would catch the workers on their way home, and finally to Jesse's boat yard, where I would sit and talk with Melvin Corl about the fish business. I didn't think I would like selling fish so much.

SACCO   The poor fish peddler.

VANZETTI   Yes, I was nothing but a poor fish peddler, Nico, but I was my own boss. Before, I used to wash dishes, dig ditches, and shovel coal in the summer and snow in the winter. But all this I did for someone else's gain.

SACCO   I know what that's like. I worked beside a man and I cannot tell you his name because the factory kept us so busy that we never had the chance to talk. He was not as fast as the rest of us but he pushed himself to keep up. When a man makes a mistake a machine doesn't have the sense to stop. It cut off his hand. The next day, there was another man in his place. That night I went home and told Rosa that we would take the family back to Italy. I had had enough. I promised her I would go and get our passports.

VANZETTI   I never thought of going back.

SACCO   Here, I can't work with the other prisoners. They won't let me because they say I'm too fast. I came to America, I paid a month's wages to have someone teach me how to run an edging machine. For almost ten years I made shoes. I worked hard. I worked fast and now I sit in this hole and I can't even get shoes that fit.

VANZETTI   The good shoemaker.

They are at the police station after having been interrogated.

SACCO   Rosa, come as quickly as you can to the police station. Something has happened. Don't worry, everything will be fine. It's all a big mistake.

VANZETTI   What did you tell them?

SACCO   Nothing.

VANZETTI   Good.

SACCO   He asked me question after question—

VANZETTI   All in English?

SACCO   Yes. It went on for hours. I needed you to explain what he was saying, I was tired and confused, I was afraid they would do to me what they did to Salsedo, I begged them to slow down.

VANZETTI   But instead they asked the questions faster and louder.

SACCO   I was scared that they knew about our involvement in the strikes and that they were accusing me of being an anarchist.

VANZETTI   It's not a crime to be an anarchist.

SACCO   In their eyes it is. But they were accusing me of murder. I didn't know it was murder. So yes, I looked guilty but for the wrong reasons.

The men return to their cells.

VANZETTI   In all my life, I have never stolen and I have never killed and I have never spilled blood.

SACCO   If the police had told me why they were questioning me then things would be different.

VANZETTI   All they saw when they looked at us were anarchist militants, political agitators, and antiwar propagandists.

SACCO   You can be all these things and not be a murderer.

VANZETTI   I am not a murderer.

SACCO   We are not murderers.

VANZETTI   Many know the truth. They are Italians, as well as Americans, and some we do not even know. Human nature is good. A defence committee rallies around us. They are fighting for the sake of justice. Thousands of our comrades protest against our imprisonment. Some work night and day to free us.

SACCO   No one listens to them.

VANZETTI   They give beyond their means and work beyond their strengths.

SACCO   Their efforts are wasted. The day those men were killed our fate was sealed.

VANZETTI   I think about that day every day.

SACCO   April 15, 1920.

VANZETTI   I remember every detail.

SACCO   I can say these words over and over again but I can never regain what I have lost.

VANZETTI   I woke up in the morning, as I did every morning, to do my usual rounds. Beltrando came with me that day, a boy of twelve, pushing a heavy cart full of fish.

SACCO   I wasn't at work that day. I went to Boston to get a passport for my family.

VANZETTI   On Cherry Street I met Mr. Scavitto, who was selling cloth for suits. He offered to sell me a piece of blue serge for cheap because it had some holes.

SACCO   I caught the seven-thirty train at Stoughton Railway Station, where I ran into Dominic.

VANZETTI   I know nothing about good clothes, so I asked him to come with me to let Alfonsina Brini see the cloth.

SACCO   I met Gatti on the street and we went to Boni's for lunch. Placido Calabrio came in and sat with us.

VANZETTI   She said the cloth was a good buy, so I gave Mr. Scavitto twelve dollars and twenty-five cents. He complained I was robbing him blind. So I gave him another fifty cents.

SACCO   On my way to the passport office, I ran into Guido Quaranta. We belonged to the same dramatic club. He had tickets for *Madame X* playing at the Tremont Theatre with the great Italian artist Mimi Aguglia.

VANZETTI   It must have been noon when I left the Brinis because I heard the whistle blowing and people hurrying home from the Cordage plant for lunch. Angelo, a man I know from Suosso's Lane, bought some codfish from me.

SACCO   Finally, I got to the Italian consulate around two and gave them the photograph of my family. Then I went home.

VANZETTI   I went down to Jesse's boat yard and talked to Luigi Falzani while he was painting his boat. I left him to his work and went home.

SACCO   April 15, 1920.

VANZETTI   I remember every person I talked to that day. How can I be in two places at one time?

SACCO   I met so many people that day. So many people remember seeing me. So many Italians.

VANZETTI   They have no case against us. We are innocent.

SACCO   All we have to do is tell the truth.

> *During the following, SACCO and VANZETTI put on their shirts, ties, and jackets.*

VANZETTI   They come and wake me up at six o'clock on our first trial day. They chain me to the guard and I go down to where the car is ready. We enter into a park, the name of which I now forget but the beauty of which I will never forget. I regret having only one pair of eyes able to look in one direction alone. Then, I find myself in front of Dedham jail, where I know you are waiting inside. After, we are brought to the court protected by numerous American Cossacks, as if we were Russian tsars.

SACCO   Going to the trial was almost like going to Barnum and Bailey's.

> *They are dressed for the court. Circus music strikes up and the trial begins.*

Hurry, hurry!

VANZETTI   Step right up!

SACCO   Right this way!

VANZETTI   Ladies and gentlemen,

SACCO   don't be shy.

VANZETTI   The trial of Nicola Sacco, the good shoemaker and Bartolomeo Vanzetti, the poor fish peddler,

SACCO   for the cold-blooded murder of Alessandro Berardelli and Frederick A. Parmenter.

VANZETTI   See the astonishing destruction of these Italian

SACCO   immigrant,

VANZETTI   anarchist

SACCO   underdogs.

VANZETTI   By their unseen and invisible adversary,

SACCO   an enemy that cannot be blamed,

VANZETTI   nor touched,

SACCO   nor stopped.

SACCO & VANZETTI   The Commonwealth of Massachusetts

SACCO   and its dark,

VANZETTI   narrow-minded agent,

SACCO   Judge Webster B. Thayer.

VANZETTI   "Wait and see what I'm going to do to those anarchist bastards."

SACCO   And in the Red corner...

"L'Internationale"[4] plays.

VANZETTI   The underdog defence attorney calls his witnesses,

VANZETTI becomes the witnesses for the defence.

SACCO   Angelo Guidobone.

VANZETTI   "I bought some fish from him. He couldn't have been in two places at once."

SACCO   Alfonsina Brini.

VANZETTI   "He is a studious man. He likes to sit and read."

SACCO   Carlos Affe.

VANZETTI   "This is crazy, that man wouldn't hurt a fly."

SACCO   Giuespeppe Andrower.

VANZETTI   "He came into the passport office that afternoon."

SACCO   Fortinato Antonello.

VANZETTI   "I sold Sacco some fruit that day. I know Sacco perfectly."

SACCO   Alberto Bosco.

VANZETTI   "He was working in Plymouth, that's about twenty-five miles away."

SACCO   Beltrando Brini.

VANZETTI   "I was working with him that day."

SACCO   Placido Calabrio.

VANZETTI   "I saw him at Boni's diner."

SACCO   Guido Quaranta.

VANZETTI   "He is a good husband and father."

SACCO   Paolucci Ceccondino.

VANZETTI   "He delivered fish to my house at ten o'clock that day."

4 Eugène Pottier and Pierre De Geyter

SACCO   Angelo Cristoforia.

VANZETTI   "He always came to work early and was one of the last to leave."

SACCO   Rocco Dalesandro.

VANZETTI   "I saw him with my own eyes on April fifteenth."

SACCO   Niccolo Gatti.

VANZETTI   "We were having lunch at Boni's diner."

SACCO   Dominic Ricci.

VANZETTI   "I saw him on the platform of Stoughton Station."

SACCO   Angelo Ricci.

VANZETTI   "My brother saw him on the platform of Stoughton Station."

SACCO   Joseph Scavitto.

VANZETTI   "He bought some cloth from me. I gave him a good deal."

SACCO   Luigi Falzani.

VANZETTI   "He came to visit me at Jesse's boat yard."

SACCO   Emielio Falcone.

VANZETTI   "No, those two don't resemble the man I saw shooting."

SACCO   Perdro Iscorla.

VANZETTI   "No, that's not him."

SACCO   Cesidio Magnarelli.

VANZETTI   "I know him and he is innocent."

SACCO   Vincenzo Testani.

VANZETTI   "It happened so fast, there is no way anyone could say who it was."

SACCO   And many,

VANZETTI   many, many more,

SACCO   who all placed

VANZETTI   the poor fish peddler

SACCO   and the good shoemaker

VANZETTI   many miles from the scene of the crime.

SACCO   And the honourable,

VANZETTI   we use that term loosely,

SACCO   Judge Webster B. Thayer presided.

VANZETTI   But what does Judge Thayer do when he hears an Italian immigrant?

SACCO   He plugs his ears and says,

VANZETTI   "I'm not listening, I'm not listening!"

SACCO   And in the red, white, and blue corner,

> *The "Star Spangled Banner"*[5] *plays. SACCO becomes KATZMANN.*

VANZETTI   The prosecutor, the lily-white Messer. Katzmann, the appalling and Lilliputian servant of the Commonwealth of Massachusetts said:

KATZMANN   I'm the meanest son of a bitch in the whole wide world, and I'm gonna have those little Italians shaking in their boots.

VANZETTI   But those little Italian anarchists didn't shake in their boots.

KATZMANN   Now Mr. Vanzetti, I am amazed that you can remember so clearly exactly where you were and what you were doing on April fifteenth, almost nine months ago today. Is your memory so clear on all the days of the year? Can you, for example, tell me exactly what you were doing on the first day of this year? How about on Washington's birthday? Or the fourth of July? Can any of us be as sure as Mr. Vanzetti here about what we do every minute of the day? Let's think back. What time did you go to bed last night? What time did you go to bed three nights ago? Where were you at *(looks at his watch)* a quarter-to-one a week ago? Where were you twenty-two days ago from today? Were you at the bank? Were you at the market? Where were you thirteen days ago? Six? What day of the week was that? With whom were you talking, if anybody, at ten-minutes-to-three thirty-four days ago from today?

5 Francis Scott Key

Do you remember? Do you? Hey?

>Pause

Mr. Vanzetti, could you perhaps be mistaken, or confused, or lying?

VANZETTI   Io non capisco. *[I do not understand.]*

KATZMANN   How convenient. Now the prosecution would like to call a few witnesses.

VANZETTI   The prosecution

KATZMANN   made its case

VANZETTI   on the astounding, mind-boggling, and wondrous eyesight

KATZMANN   of several concerned citizens.

>*VANZETTI becomes the witnesses for the prosecution.*

Austin Reed.

VANZETTI   "Although I saw them from thirty feet away, from a window sixty feet above their heads, for only about three seconds, it was them... I think."

KATZMANN   Mary E. Splaine.

VANZETTI   "He had dark eyebrows but his complexion was white, a peculiar white that looked greenish. I'm almost sure it's him. I could be mistaken."

KATZMANN   Lewis Wade.

VANZETTI   "That's him. Portuguese, Italian... I don't know, they all look the same to me. I could tell he was a foreigner because of the way he ran. They're all a little unsteady."

KATZMANN   Frank Pelser.

VANZETTI   "Well I wouldn't say it was him, but he's a dead image of the man I seen. Well I know I said I saw him put the last shot in Berardelli, but to tell you the truth, I heard shooting when I was at the window and then I hid under a bench. I only told a falsehood because I don't like to go to court."

KATZMANN   Georgina Brown.

VANZETTI   "Well the car was moving really fast, but he was five foot six and one hundred sixty-five pounds. He had medium-length hair and black eyebrows. I distinctly remember his hands. They were big, like killer big."

KATZMANN   James F. Bostock.

VANZETTI   "Well I don't know as I could really describe the bandits. They were swarthy, dark complected, I thought they were Italian fruit peddlers."

KATZMANN   Emerging from the shadows of the truth comes the star witness for the prosecution, Miss Lola Andrews.

VANZETTI   "Well let me see now, umm… Julia and I, well, we were… uhhh… we were lost… yeah, yeah, that's right, we were lost. So we saw these guys, these, like, Mafia guys hanging out by their car, and we asked them for directions. They were really nice to us but they couldn't really speak English so they couldn't help us. They had dark hair. That's them right over there."

KATZMANN   Are you sure?

VANZETTI   "There is no doubt in my mind." *(giggles)*

KATZMANN   I have been a prosecutor, gentlemen, for more than eleven years now, and I cannot recall in that long service for the Commonwealth that ever before have I laid eyes on or given ear to so convincing and so lovely a witness as Lola Andrews.

> *Lola giggles.*

Nicola Sacco, did you leave this country during the war to go to Mexico? What were you doing there? Don't you think going away from your country is a vulgar thing to do when she needs you? Do you think it is a brave thing to do? Do you think it would be a brave thing to go away from your wife when she needed you? You say you don't believe in war. What do you believe in? Anarchy? Communism? Robbery? Murder?

VANZETTI   *(interrupting the circus)* Sacco is a worker from his boyhood, a skilled worker, a lover of work, with a good job and pay, a bank account, a good and lovely wife, two beautiful children, and a neat little home on the verge of a wood near a brook. Sacco is a heart, a faith, a character, a man, a lover of nature, and of mankind. A man who gave all, who sacrificed all—money, rest, mundane ambitions, his own wife, his children, himself, and his own life—for the cause of liberty and his love of mankind. Sacco has never dreamt to steal, never to assassinate. Never.

SACCO   And the questions went on for days, over two thousand questions, all of them obtuse, stupid, leading,

VANZETTI   and all in English.

SACCO and VANZETTI take the stand, speaking with accents.

No, I do not understand...

SACCO   No…. Yes…. No.

VANZETTI   What is that you say?

SACCO   Ah…

VANZETTI   Uh…

SACCO & VANZETTI   Yes.

SACCO   Give me chance to explain.

VANZETTI   I cannot answer in one word.

SACCO   Your, Your Honour...

VANZETTI   Come prego? *[Pardon?]*

SACCO   Io non capisco. *[I do not understand.]*

VANZETTI   Prego un'altra volta? *[Could you repeat that, please?]*

SACCO   Io non capisco. *[I do not understand.]*

VANZETTI   And the circus went on like this.

SACCO   Thirty-eight days into the trial the *New York World* newspaper puts it in black and white: "Are they Guilty or Not Guilty?"

Patriotic music plays under KATZMANN's speech.

KATZMANN   The question is one of fact, gentlemen, arrived at under the rules of law. It has been said to you that your decision will take away the lives of two men, if it be that of guilty. Let me assure you that you are not taking away the lives of the defendants by finding them guilty of a murder of which they are guilty, the law takes their lives away and not you. It is for you to say if they are guilty and you are done. You pronounce no sentence of death. The question of where the truth lies here is a cold proposition of fact that is to be decided without any regard to those who may be deprived of a friend, a husband, or a father by your decision, for no regard was given for Mrs. Berardelli and Mrs. Parmenter. You are the consultants here, gentlemen, the twelve of you, and these parties come to you and ask you to find what the truth is on the two issues of guilt or innocence. Gentlemen of the jury, do your duty. Do it like men. Stand together you men of Norfolk!

> *The patriotic music has reached a crescendo. The sound of a gavel stops the music. Silence.*

VANZETTI   The carefully selected and non-judgmental jury said,

KATZMANN   Italian immigrant anarchists? Oh yes, they're guilty.

VANZETTI   Judge Thayer said,

SACCO   "Oh yes, they're guilty."

VANZETTI   The governor said,

SACCO   "Oh yes, they're guilty."

VANZETTI   The president said,

SACCO   "Oh yes, they're guilty."

VANZETTI   The *Boston Herald* said,

SACCO   "Oh yes, they're guilty."

VANZETTI   We are innocent.

SACCO   You kill two innocent men!

VANZETTI   Courage! Courage!

SACCO   Sono innocente! *[We are innocent!]*

VANZETTI   Couragio. *[Courage.]*

SACCO   Couragio. *[Courage.]*

SACCO & VANZETTI   *(to each other)* Comrade.

VANZETTI   And so the poor fish peddler and the good shoemaker were found guilty and started to wait,

SACCO   and wait,

VANZETTI   and wait to hear what was to be their fate.

They return to their cells. Their accents are gone. SACCO paces, while VANZETTI writes.

SACCO   One, two, three, four… *(He turns around and paces back.)* One, two, three, four…. One, two, three, four…

VANZETTI   Nico.

SACCO   One, two, three, four…. One, two, three—

VANZETTI   Nico.

SACCO   I'm always in this narrow, sad cell walking up and down, up and down. Thinking about everything all at once, so many images crowd my mind.

VANZETTI   I will work, I will read, and I will write.

SACCO   Not a day has passed when I do not think of Rosa, Dante, and Ines. They are always in my memory, and I think sometimes it must be easier for me because I am not the one who is being left behind. I am tired, tired, tired.

VANZETTI   Continue the good war… the war that knows neither fear nor scruples, neither pity nor truce.

SACCO   Every night before I fall asleep, I believe I will wake up and none of this will have happened. But today, before I even opened my eyes, I knew I wasn't in my bed and that Rosa was not beside me. I could smell the musty air of this dank place, and when I finally opened them, I was not surprised to see the same old wall looking back at me.

VANZETTI   I am trying hard to finish this book, *The Rise of American Civilization.* I find it difficult. I can only read at night and the bars on my window cast shadows on the pages. It is strange, but I feel compelled to finish it.

SACCO   Rosa asked me to describe my prison life to her. It upset her so much that I have not told her what it is really like since.

VANZETTI   I still believe in the America of my youth but I haven't found it yet.

SACCO   Because it doesn't exist.

VANZETTI   Then how would you explain Beltrando? He is going to Harvard this year. The son of poor Italian immigrants like us—factory workers.

SACCO   And how many won't go to Harvard, or any school? Most of them will end up like their parents, struggling to put food on the table and a roof over their heads.

VANZETTI   At the age of twelve, with the money he earned picking blueberries, he bought a violin. I remember when we walked to the shop, he didn't say a word, but I could see his hand in his pocket clutching his savings. Now he is teaching violin to eleven pupils in Plymouth.

SACCO   He is only one immigrant.

VANZETTI   Perhaps Dante will have the chance to live in the America of our dreams.

SACCO   Did the men for whom the monument on Bunker Hill was built fight for that same America? "All men are created equal."[6] If the man who wrote those words could have been in that courtroom, what would he have thought?

VANZETTI   The conscience of the people of Massachusetts must be awakened. Working people, underdogs, Reds, know instinctively what is going on. The same thing has happened before. But the average law-admiring, authority-respecting citizen does not know. All that is needed is that the facts of the case be generally known.

SACCO   The faces of men who have been a long time in jail have a peculiar frozen look under the eyes. The face of a man who has been a long time in jail never loses that tightness under the eyes.

VANZETTI   Everyone must work to that end, no matter what happens, that the facts of the case may be known so that no one can plead ignorance. Everyone in the state, everyone in the country, will carry the burden of guilt. So that no one can say, "I would have protested but I didn't know what was being done."

SACCO   I sit looking at the sick flesh of my hands—hands that haven't worked for seven years.

6 *The Declaration of Independence*, Thomas Jefferson

VANZETTI   I ask, if to live for the love of life and not for heroism or wisdom is cowardice. I am ready and will not die as a rabbit or a worm. Italy is weeping tears of blood.

SACCO   Do you know how long a year is? How many months there are in a year? How many weeks there are in a month? How many days there are in a week?

VANZETTI   The socialist is feared by the liberal, the democrat, and the republican, while they fear the communist, who fears the socialist and the liberal and the democrat, while the anarchist distrusts them all.

SACCO   Do you know how many hours there are in a day?

VANZETTI   The Italian king dislikes the pope, the pope the king. The king dislikes Mussolini, and Mussolini is a slave to the capitalists.

SACCO   When a day is twenty-three hours on a cot in a cell. In a cell, in a row of cells, in a tier of rows of cells, all empty with the choked emptiness of dreams?

VANZETTI   But what of the great masses in the fields, the shops, the studios, the army, corrupted by thousands of years of slavery, poverty, ignorance, unspeakable suffering...

SACCO   Do you know the dreams of men in jail?

VANZETTI   *(enraptured)* O, the blessed green of the wilderness and of the open land. O, the blue vastness of the oceans, the fragrance of the flowers, and the sweetness of the fruits, the sky reflecting lakes, the singing torrents, the telling brooks. O, the valleys, the hills, the Alps! O, the mystic dawn, the glory of the moon. O, the sunset, the twilight, carry us from our cells to the open horizon under the sun at daytime, under the stars at night.

> *The lights pulse.*
>
> *Perhaps some of the Woody Guthrie song "Old Judge Thayer" plays as the two men wait in their cells.*

I am a poor fish peddler.

SACCO   I am a good shoemaker.

VANZETTI   I am an immigrant.

SACCO   I am an Italian.

VANZETTI   I am an anarchist.

SACCO   I am a prisoner.

VANZETTI   I am waiting.

SACCO   Waiting.

VANZETTI   Twenty-eight seasons,

SACCO   seven springs, seven summers,

VANZETTI   seven falls, seven winters,

SACCO   seven rings on a tree,

VANZETTI   seven birthdays,

SACCO   seven Christmases,

VANZETTI   eighty-four months,

SACCO   three hundred and sixty-four weeks.

VANZETTI   How old were you when you came to America?

SACCO   Seventeen.

VANZETTI   I was twenty. A young man.

SACCO   Now I am thirty-six.

VANZETTI   I am thirty-nine.

SACCO   Waiting

VANZETTI   for seven years,

SACCO   four months,

VANZETTI   and eleven days,

SACCO   to be exact.

VANZETTI   A long,

SACCO   long,

VANZETTI   long,

SACCO   wait.

VANZETTI   For what? Found guilty of first-degree murder, for which the penalty is death.

SACCO   We wait

VANZETTI   for the wheels of justice to turn, slowly. The case is appealed not once,

SACCO   but five times. People come forward admitting to perjury.

VANZETTI   Judge Thayer is charged with prejudice against us.

SACCO   New evidence is produced.

A memory in prison, November 1925.

I thought he was playing a trick. I didn't listen. I didn't trust him. He came up to me before in the courtyard and said, "Nic, I know who did the murders." I walked away.

VANZETTI   What do you mean?

SACCO   He said it to me in the courtyard. He said, "Nic, I know who done the job."

VANZETTI   What job?

SACCO   He sent me a map showing me the crime, I tore it up. He whispered to me underneath my window, "I know who done the job." I ignored him at first. I thought he was an informer.

VANZETTI   Nic, no one is spying on you.

SACCO   I was thinking he was like Carbone, sitting in the cell next to mine for four years listening to everything I say. Always whispering with the guard after my visits with Rosa, asking me questions about the robbery and the bombings. I would always tell Carbone the same thing, that I am an anarchist, that I am against the capitalist, but that I have never killed any man. But this man, he is different.

VANZETTI   Nic, are you eating?

SACCO   Yes, but I still believe they are putting something in our food. There is a metallic taste to the meat.

VANZETTI   Nic, we've talked about this. No one is trying to poison you, and Carbone was never spying on you.

SACCO   There is a constant humming that comes from under my bed and a smell in my cell, which leads me to believe they are putting something in the air. I've tried to tell Rosa but she just cries and tells me I'm tired. Something must be done.

VANZETTI   You should listen to Rosa and get some rest.

SACCO   He said he'd seen Rosa and the children come so many times to see me. How happy we were together.

VANZETTI   Carbone was not an informer, you know that.

SACCO   No, no, not Carbone. I'm talking about Madeiros.

VANZETTI   Madeiros?

SACCO   Celestino Madeiros. He's a boy, eighteen, an apprentice to the Morellis.

VANZETTI   What did he say?

SACCO   He smuggled a confession to me in a magazine. He wrote it on a piece of paper and it fell out at my feet.

VANZETTI   Where is this piece of paper? Where is this confession?

SACCO pulls out a piece of paper.

What does it say?

SACCO   I hereby confess to being in the South Braintree Shoe Company crime and Sacco and Vanzetti were not involved in this crime. Celestino F. Madeiros.

VANZETTI   Nic, is this true?

SACCO   I've always said it was a professional job. Madeiros says that the Morellis needed an extra man.

VANZETTI   Why would he do this now? Why would he sign his name to a piece of paper that would kill him?

SACCO   Guilty conscience. He felt sorry for my family.

VANZETTI   No one will believe this.

SACCO   I showed it to Mr. Thompson. He has met with Madeiros and tells me that the court will grant us a retrial.

VANZETTI   If Parmenter and Berardelli came back from the dead, the state of Massachusetts would still find us guilty.

SACCO   They will have to listen to us.

VANZETTI   Will they?

SACCO   How can they not?

VANZETTI   ...the Morellis?

SACCO   The police in Providence and New Bedford know them as professional criminals. Madeiros said there were five of them in the car. He described everything. The only thing he won't give are names.

VANZETTI   What was he doing in jail?

SACCO   He's been found guilty of first-degree murder committed at a bank robbery. The man is a professional highway robber and his record is terrifying.

VANZETTI   Why would they believe a man already convicted and about to undergo the penalty of death? His confession won't mean anything.

SACCO   Compare his case with ours: he is an habitual robber, we were two hard workers with a good reputation, he has a bad record, ours were spotless, his conduct in prison was bad, we were publicly declared "model prisoners." There is no doubt of his guilt, whereas there are many doubts about our guilt. The state has not a single testimony to prove that you have been seen at the crime—you have never been there, we were never there.

VANZETTI   Nico, remember that in their eyes we are not only murderers and robbers but Italian anarchists as well.

SACCO   If the retrial is fair, we have a chance.

VANZETTI   It was not what we did but who we are that convicted us.

SACCO   It means we will be free.

VANZETTI   We have been disappointed so many times already.

SACCO   This is our last chance.

VANZETTI   But Nico—

SACCO   Please… we can't give up. If we stop now they've won.

VANZETTI   I want to believe you.

SACCO   This confession proves our innocence. They have no reason to keep us here any longer. Think of all of our comrades who have stood by us all this time. They have formed committees, written petitions, and rallied against the government. All for us. If we give up, if we don't pursue this, we have betrayed them. How can they fight for us if we won't fight for ourselves?

VANZETTI   We must do all that we can.

SACCO   Think of Rosa's face when she sees me—a free man.

VANZETTI   They will have to tell the world that they put two innocent men in prison.

SACCO   I will sit down at my own table with my family.

VANZETTI   I will travel the world telling our story.

SACCO   We will meet again.

VANZETTI   Face to face.

SACCO & VANZETTI   Comrade.

> *The circus music plays again but it is warped.*

SACCO   See the amazing spectacle of "The Pinko Commie Wops,"

VANZETTI   on yet another ride on the "Wheels of Justice,"

SACCO   towards their inevitable destination

SACCO & VANZETTI   "Old Sparky!"

> *An electrical pulsing sound. VANZETTI becomes Judge THAYER.*

SACCO   *(reading)* I hereby confess

THAYER   Unreliable.

SACCO   to being in the South Braintree Shoe Company crime

THAYER   Untrustworthy.

SACCO   and Sacco and Vanzetti were not involved in this crime.

THAYER   Untrue.

SACCO   Celestino F. Madeiros.

THAYER   Sketchy and inconsistent. Motion denied.

SACCO   But he confessed.

THAYER   Motion denied.

SACCO   He said it wasn't us.

THAYER   Motion denied.

> *The circus music comes to a halt.*

Madeiros is, without doubt, a crook, a thief, a robber, a liar, a rum-runner, a bouncer in a house of ill fame, a smuggler, and a man who has been convicted and sentenced to death for the murder of a cashier at the Wrentham bank. An affidavit from a man of this type must be examined and scrutinized with the greatest possible care, caution, and judgment before the verdict of a jury approved by the supreme judicial court of this Commonwealth is set aside. It is popularly supposed he confessed to committing this crime. In his testimony to me he could not recall the details or describe the neighbourhood. He furthermore stated that the government had double-crossed him and he proposes to double-cross the government. I am not impressed with his knowledge of the South Braintree murders. I give no weight to the Madeiros confession.

SACCO   I don't believe it. I don't believe it.

VANZETTI   Now it is obvious to all that the judge and the system are prejudiced against us. When even the society itself, the people, believe in our innocence, the state still wants our death. I cannot resist the will of the state. Our struggle has always been fated to end this way.

SACCO   We are lost.

> *The two men are back in their cells. VANZETTI resumes writing. SACCO lies on his cot.*

VANZETTI   Sometimes in my solitude, I think the world is gradually forgetting this son who has been entombed alive, but I will bear my cross. There are those who will never forget me.

SACCO   Still living at the same hotel, the same room, and the same old number fourteen. I don't want to see anyone. Tell everyone to leave me alone. I don't want their help. I'm not here to relieve their guilt.

VANZETTI   Please excuse poor Nic for certain acts or words. You must understand that he benefits from the love of his friends, even if he seems to not feel or perceive it.

SACCO   They told me if I didn't eat they would feed me through a tube. I was too weak and could not fight them so I said, I will eat. I stopped the hunger strike because there was no sign of life in me. Life begins to revive slowly and calmly, but yet without a horizon and always with sadness and visions of death.

VANZETTI   Yesterday, Mr. Thompson was here and told me the judge has set a date for the sentence. I look forward to seeing you, as Mr.

Thompson has assured me that we will be together after the sentence has been passed. It has been a long time without seeing you, comrade.

SACCO   I was thinking that after all these long years apart, it will be good to sit down with you face to face and talk, even if it will be our last days. Regarding our sentence, I have no idea because the experiences of the past years have taught us not to delude ourselves anymore.

VANZETTI   I met with the governor. He is conducting an inquiry into our case. We had a good talk and he gave me a good and hearty handshake at the parting.

SACCO   We don't even believe in government and yet we are forced to plead with them. If man was free to make his own decisions… if the government was abolished, if institutions did not exist…

VANZETTI   Nic, our case is this, we were found guilty of first-degree murder and the penalty is death.

SACCO   It is the end of the struggle and I hope it is so.

VANZETTI   Now that the State Supreme Court has denied us a new trial, our sentence will be served. I am told that only now can we obtain executive clemency, which means the grace of Governor Fuller, to change our sentence from death to life imprisonment. Let everyone know that we prefer death to the chains—that not a word should be said, not a cent given, nor a finger raised, if not to give us freedom or death.

SACCO   Freedom or death.

SACCO & VANZETTI   Freedom or death.

> *SACCO and VANZETTI put on their jackets. They step forward to hear their sentencing. The men speak with Italian accents in their speeches to the court.*

SACCO   I am no orator. It is not very familiar with me, the English language, and as I know, as my friend has told me, my comrade, Vanzetti, will speak more long, so I thought to give him the chance. I never knew, never heard, even read in history anything so cruel as this court. After seven years prosecuting, you still consider us guilty. And these gentle people here are arrayed with us in this courtroom. I know the sentence will be between two classes, the oppressed class and the rich class, there will always be collision between the one and the other. We fraternize the people with the books, with the literature. You persecute the people, tyrannize them, and kill them. We try the education of people always. You try to put a path between us and some other nationality that hates each other. That is why I am here today on this bench, for having been of the oppressed class. Well you are the oppressor, you know it, Judge Thayer, you know all my life, you know why I have been here, and after seven years that you have been persecuting me and my poor wife, you still today sentence us to death. I would like to tell all my life, but what is the use? You know all about what I say before, that is, my comrade, Vanzetti, will be talking more long because he is more familiar with the language and I will give him the chance. My comrade, the kind man to all the children, you know he is innocent. You forget all this population that has been with us for seven years, to sympathize and give us all their energy and all their kindness. You do not care for them. And I want to thank you all, you peoples, my comrades, who have been with me for seven years, with the Sacco-Vanzetti case, and I will give my friend a chance.

> *VANZETTI tugs at SACCO's arm and whispers in his ear,*
> *SACCO resumes.*

I forget one thing, which my comrade remember me. As I said before, Judge Thayer knows all my life and he knows that I am never guilty, never—not yesterday, or today, nor forever.

VANZETTI   What I say is that I am innocent. In all my life I have never stolen and I have never killed and I have never spilled blood. That is what I want to say. And it is not all. Not only am I innocent of these crimes, not only in all my life have I never stolen, never killed, never spilled blood, but I have struggle all my life, since I began to reason, to eliminate crime from the earth. Everybody that knows these two arms knows very well that I did not need to go into the streets and kill a man or try to take money. I can live by my two hands and live well. I have refused to go in business because I understand that business is a speculation on profit upon certain people that must depend upon the businessman, and I do not consider that that is right and therefore I refuse to do that. I struggled all my life to eliminate crimes—the exploitation and the oppression of the man by the man, and if there is a reason why I am here as a guilty man, if there is a reason why in a few minutes that you can doom me, it is this and none else. What we have suffered during these seven years no human tongue can say, and yet you see me before you, not trembling, you see me looking you in your eyes straight, not blushing, not changing colour, not ashamed or in fear. We were tried during a time whose character has now passed into history. A time when there was an hysteria of resentment and hate against the people of our principles, against the foreigner. I am glad to be on the doomed scaffold if I can say to mankind— "All that they say to you, all that they have promised to you, it was a lie, it was an illusion, it was a cheat, it was a fraud, it was a crime. They promised you liberty. Where is liberty? They promised you prosperity. Where is prosperity? They have promised you elevation. Where is the elevation?" Well I will say that I not only am not guilty of these two crimes—though some sins, but not crimes. I have never stolen and I have never killed and I have never spilled blood and I have fought against crime, and I fought, and I have sacrificed myself even to eliminate the crimes that the law and the church legitimate and sanctify. This is what I say: I would not wish to a dog or to a snake, to the most low and misfortunate creature of the earth—I would not wish to any of them what I have had to suffer for things that I am not guilty of. I am suffering because I am a radical—and indeed I am a radical; I have suffered because I was an Italian, and indeed I am an Italian; I have suffered more for my family and for my beloved than for myself; but I am so convinced to be right, that you can only kill me once, but if you could execute me two times and if I could be reborn two other times, I would live again to do what I have done already. I have finished. Thank you.

They take a step forward to receive the sentence.

VOICE   It is considered and ordered by the court that you, Nicola Sacco, suffer the punishment of death by the passage of a current of electricity through your body within the week beginning on Sunday, the twenty-second of August in the year of our Lord, one thousand, nine hundred and twenty-seven. This is the sentence of the law.

It is considered by the court that you, Bartolomeo Vanzetti, suffer the punishment—

VANZETTI   *(overlapping)* Wait a minute, please, Your Honour. May I speak for a moment with my lawyer, Mr. Thompson?

VOICE   of death by the passage of a current of electricity through your body within the week beginning on Sunday, the twenty-second of August, in the year of our Lord, one thousand, nine hundred and twenty-seven. This is the sentence of the law.

SACCO   You know I am innocent. That is the same words I pronounced seven years ago.

VANZETTI   You condemn two innocent men.

The men return to their cells. Their accents are gone.

SACCO   It is very sad to be doomed and waiting for the electric chair. I am still alive and how I live I do not know. We live, as always, in struggle.

VANZETTI   Governor Fuller is a murderer, as are the other politicians, as is Thayer, Katzmann, the state perjurers, and all the others. He shook hands with me like a brother, made me believe he was honestly intentioned. His conviction will not make us guilty—we are, and will remain, innocent, our execution will be the same as murder, our blood will call for revenge.

SACCO   Waiting.

VANZETTI   For the system to decide it will strap us into a wooden chair, put electrodes on our legs and heads, attach metal caps to our shaved skulls, ask us if we have any last words, and pull a mask over our faces. And then run twenty-four hundred volts of electricity through our bodies for seven seconds, followed by six-hundred volts for seventeen seconds, and repeat this for five minutes until the doctor says if we are dead or not.

SACCO   *(writing)* My dear Rosa,

Governor Fuller's decision made clear what I knew all along—the execution date has been set: August 23, 1927. We die for anarchy.

VANZETTI   And our hands have turned red and then white, the cords of our necks have stood out like steel bands, our eyeballs have popped out, and our flesh has swollen and burned, and our skin has stretched to the point of breaking…

SACCO   *(writing)* My dear Ines,

I will bring with me your little and so dearest letter and carry it right under my heart to the last day of my life. When I die, it will be buried with your father who loves you so much, as I do also your brother Dante and holy, dear mother.

VANZETTI   We are proud for death and fall as only the anarchist can fall.

SACCO   *(writing)* My dear Dante, son and companion,

Since the day I saw you last, I had always the idea to write you
this letter. If nothing happens, they will electrocute us right after
midnight...

> *Perhaps the sound of Woody Guthrie's song "Sacco's Letter to
> his Son" plays. The men remove their coats, vests, jewellery,
> and prepare for the chair. They turn to each other, shake hands
> as when they first met. Holding hands, they walk up centre,
> turn, hug, go into their cells, set up chairs, which up till now
> have been cots, and they sit. There is a surge of electrical sound
> and an intense flickering of lights. Suddenly a loud pop, as if a
> fuse has been blown, and a bright white light illuminates each
> of them.*

VANZETTI   Had it not been for these things, I might have lived out
my life talking at street corners to scorning men. I might have died
unmarked, unknown, a failure. Now we are not failures. This is our
career and our triumph. Never in our full lives could we hope to
do such work for tolerance, for justice, for man's understanding of
man as now we do by accident. Our words—our lives—our pains—
nothing! The taking of our lives—lives of a good shoemaker and a
poor fish peddler— All! This last moment belongs to us. This agony
is our triumph.

SACCO   True wisdom is tolerance.

VANZETTI   I want a roof for every family, bread for every mouth,
education for every heart, and light for every intellect.

SACCO   I am convinced that human history has not yet begun, that we
find ourselves in the last period of the prehistoric.

VANZETTI   The supreme goal of life is happiness.

SACCO   My happiness is the happiness of all.

VANZETTI   We seek our liberty in the liberty of all. This is our career
and our triumph...

SACCO   Seven years,

VANZETTI   four months,

SACCO   and eleven days of struggle.

VANZETTI   Friends and comrades, now that the tragedy of this trial is at an end, be of one heart.

SACCO   Only two of us will die.

VANZETTI   Our ideal, you, our comrades, will live by the millions, we have won.

SACCO   Just treasure our suffering, our sorrow, our mistakes, our defeats, our passion for future battles.

VANZETTI   Be all as of one heart in this blackest hour of our tragedy. And have heart.

SACCO   Salute for us all the friends and comrades of the earth.

VANZETTI   We embrace you all and bid you our extreme goodbye with our hearts filled with love and affection.

SACCO   Now and ever, long life to you all, long life to liberty.

VANZETTI   Yours in life and death,

SACCO   Sacco.

> *The light goes out on SACCO and he shouts.*

Viva l'anarchia!

VANZETTI   Vanzetti.

> *Fade to black.*
>
> *The End*

HISTORICAL NOTES

- Between 1880 and 1920, four million Italian immigrants crossed the Atlantic to the United States. The majority of immigrants were males between the ages of twenty-four and forty-five. Many expected to stay in the United States only long enough to earn money to improve their family situation. Others intended to send for their families as soon as they could.

- Shortly after the end of World War I and the Bolshevik Revolution in Russia, the Red Scare took hold in the United States. A nationwide fear of communists, socialists, anarchists, and other dissidents suddenly grabbed the American psyche in 1919 following a series of anarchist bombings. People were jailed for expressing their views, civil liberties were ignored, and many Americans feared that a Bolshevik-style revolution was at hand.

- The Bolshevik Revolution was the culmination of events, which led to the overthrow of the Russian government in the fall of 1917. Russia had entered World War I (1914–18) in 1914, and by 1917 the country was facing hardships, including shortages of food and fuel. The people had lost faith in the war effort; they were no longer willing to send young men into battle only to be killed. The Bolsheviks were an extremist faction within the Russian Social Democratic Labour Party (later renamed the Russian Communist Party) who seized control of the government and ushered in the Soviet age.

- According to Paul Avrich, three common perspectives united anarchists. American anarchists wanted to abolish the state and destroy the power of most established institutions; they wanted the stateless society to be based upon voluntary co-operation; and they feared and combated most forms of Marxist socialism, particularly the communist model, with its reliance on centralized state authority to carry out the class aims of the proletariat.

- In 1919, Woodrow Wilson appointed a new attorney general, A. Mitchell Palmer, a Pennsylvania attorney with liberal credentials, including past support for workers' rights and womens' suffrage. Palmer, however, reversed his views. In April, the post office discovered thirty-eight bombs that had been mailed to leading American politicians and capitalists. Shortly thereafter, an Italian anarchist was blown up outside Palmer's residence. The nation's top law-enforcement official became convinced that a radical plot was underway.

- Despite finding no credible evidence that a communist plot was underway, Palmer staged more raids in January 1920. With the assistance of local law-enforcement officials throughout the country, as many as six thousand suspects were arrested and detained.

- During the afternoon of April 15, 1920, Frederick Parmenter, a paymaster, and Alessandro Beradelli, a security guard, were murdered during a robbery of fifteen thousand, seven hundred seventy-six dollars and fifty-one cents from the Slater & Morrill Shoe Company.

- The arrest of Sacco and Vanzetti coincided with the period in America known as the Red Scare, 1919–20. While neither of them had any previous criminal record, they were long recognized by the authorities and their communities as anarchist militants who had been extensively involved in labour strikes, political agitation, and antiwar propaganda.

- After a six-week trial, the jury found Sacco and Vanzetti guilty of robbery and murder on July 14, 1921. This verdict marked, however, only the beginning of a lengthy legal struggle to save the two men. It extended until 1927, during which time the defence made many separate motions, appeals, and petitions to both state and federal courts in an attempt to gain a new trial.

- On August 23, 1927, Sacco and Vanzetti, still maintaining their innocence, were executed in the electric chair.

- On Sunday, August 28, 1927, over two hundred thousand people lined the streets to watch the funeral procession. Between seven and eight thousand marched wearing scarlet arm bands that read: "Remember, Justice Crucified."

- In the two decades that followed their execution, Sacco and Vanzetti were eulogized in one hundred and forty-four poems, six plays, eight novels, the now classic portraits by Ben Shahn, and an album by Woody Guthrie.

- Fifty years later, on August 23, 1977, Michael S. Dukakis, the Governor of Massachusetts, issued a proclamation, stating that August 23 would be "Nicola Sacco and Bartolomeo Vanzetti Memorial Day," and declared that any stigma and disgrace should be forever removed from their names and from the names of their families and descendants.

- *Sacco and Vanzetti*, a documentary film by Peter Miller was released in 2007, on the eightieth anniversary of their execution.

NOTES

Comrades is inspired by *The Letters of Sacco and Vanzetti*, edited by Marion D. Frankfurter and Gardner Jackson (1928). This book was given to us by Charlie Tomlinson, who suggested that Sacco and Vanzetti be the subject of a new play.

The play is based on the lives of Nicola Sacco and Bartolomeo Vanzetti, two Italian immigrant anarchists. Both men arrived in the United States in 1908.

In the play, Sacco and Vanzetti are in separate cells in separate prisons. Although they communicate through letters, it is as if they are having a dialogue. During the flashback scenes, the men can move freely about the space and interact with one another.

Sacco and Vanzetti only speak with accents when indicated in the script.

The men should remain on stage for the entire play, flowing easily from one scene to the next and from character to character. Costume changes are not necessary.

In each cell there is a cot which the men are able to transform into electric chairs.

The voice that sentences Sacco and Vanzetti and the radio broadcast may be recorded.

The play should be performed without an intermission.

photo by David Spowart

Beth Graham was born in Antigonish, Nova Scotia, and raised in Cochrane, Alberta. She is a graduate of the University of Alberta's BFA acting program, where she met Daniela Vlaskalic and Charlie Tomlinson. Their play *The Drowning Girls* has been produced across Canada and internationally. Other co-creations include *The Vanishing Point*, *Mules*, and *Victor and Victoria's Terrifying Tale of Terrible Things*. Beth also wrote *The Gravitational Pull of Bernice Trimble* which was co-produced by Obsidian Theatre and Factory Theatre and subsequently produced at Theatre Network in Edmonton. She lives in Edmonton with her husband Patrick and their twelve-pound Pomeranian cross, Oscar.

Charlie Tomlinson lives and works in Newfoundland.

photo by David Spowart

Daniela is an actor, writer, and producer. Since graduating from the University of Alberta with a Bachelor of Fine Arts in Acting, she has worked extensively in numerous theatres across the country. Daniela began collaborating with Beth Graham and Charlie Tomlinson in 1999 with *The Drowning Girls* and has continued collaborating with Beth on several plays including, *Comrades*, *The Vanishing Point*, and *Mules*. Daniela lives in Toronto, Canada.

Fourth printing: July 2018
Printed and bound in Canada by Imprimerie Gauvin, Gatineau

Back Cover: Beth Graham, photograph by Trudie Lee
Back Cover: Kevin Corey and Nathan Cuckow, photograph by Meryl Smith Lawton
Front Cover: Photograph by Micheline Courtemanche
Production Editor and Cover Design: Micheline Courtemanche

**PLAYWRIGHTS
CANADA PRESS**

202-269 Richmond St. W.
Toronto, ON
M5V 1X1

416.703.0013
info@playwrightscanada.com
playwrightscanada.com

MIX
Paper from
responsible sources
FSC® C100212
FSC
www.fsc.org